Conrad Bonifazi

a
theology
of
things

A STUDY OF MAN IN HIS
PHYSICAL ENVIRONMENT

GREENWOOD PRESS, PUBLISHERS
WESTPORT, CONNECTICUT

Library of Congress Cataloging in Publication Data

Bonifazi, Conrad, 1912-
   A theology of things.

     Reprint of the ed. published by Lippincott, Philadel-
phia.
     Includes bibliographical references and index.
     1. Philosophy of nature. 2. Nature (Theology)
I. Title.
[BD581.B587 1976]   210   76-7549
ISBN 0-8371-8838-5

"Anthem for St. Matthew's Day" by W. H. Auden on pages 201–202 is printed with the kind permission of Mr. Auden. It was originally composed for the patronal festival of St. Matthew's Church, Northampton, England.

Copyright © 1967 by Conrad Bonifazi.

Originally published in 1967 by J. B. Lippincott Company, Philadelphia

This edition published by arrangement with J. B. Lippincott Company, Philadelphia, New York.

Reprinted in 1976 by Greenwood Press,
a division of Williamhouse-Regency Inc.

Library of Congress Catalog Card Number 76-7549

ISBN 0-8371-8838-5

Printed in the United States of America

For Laurella and Nicola

Acknowledgements

In bringing to completion this work of several years I gratefully acknowledge the readiness of my wife, Laurella, to submit many of her interests to its demands, and her help in transcribing the material at various stages of its growth. I also wish to thank my colleague Dr. Charles S. McCoy, of the Pacific School of Religion, for his kindness in reading the manuscript, and for the encouragement of his criticism.

CONRAD BONIFAZI

Pacific School of Religion
Berkeley, California
June 1966

Contents

Introduction: A Waiting Universe

At no time was it ever more thrilling and enjoyable to be a poet and to be alive, when the life of the whole planet is triggered off by a hair, when every moment is as precious as bread and wine, when the rumble and roar of Chaos challenges us for every atom of faith, hope and courage, in a measure which our Maker has never before done us the honour of expecting from His creatures.
                                        Roy Campbell [1]

The religious significance of the inorganic is immense, but it is rarely considered by theology. In most theological discussions the general term "nature" covers all particular dimensions of the "natural." This is one of the reasons why the quantitatively overwhelming realm of the inorganic has had such a strong anti-religious impact on many people in the ancient and modern worlds. A "theology of the inorganic" is lacking.
                                        Paul Tillich [2]

How can Christianity call itself catholic if the universe itself is left out?
                                        Simone Weil [3]

THE FERMENT OF RELIGIOUS THINKING in our time has been greatly accelerated by the discovery of the immensity and the unity of the world about us and within us. The

[1] Concluding paragraph of the unpublished introduction to his translation of Horace's *Art of Poetry*, in the care of Henry Regnery Co., Chicago.

[2] *Systematic Theology*, III (Chicago: University of Chicago Press, 1963), p. 18.

[3] *Waiting on God* (London: Fontana, 1959), p. 116.

11

physical sciences extend the abysses of time and space, establishing new relationships between the universe and ourselves, while those disciplines that explore the private time-space of the mind permit us glimpses of the bottomless abyss whence self-awareness takes its rise and into which it sinks. Between inner and outer worlds the network of living relationships becomes ever more fine-spun and complex, and there, enmeshed by fascination and anxiety, by a sense of answerableness and a desire for life, man seeks to understand the nature of his destiny.

Unfortunately, everyone is not constitutionally capable of affirming life with the verve and relish of the poet Roy Campbell. Sensitive persons, alarmed by this agitation and attraction, and theologians who feel responsible for their particular interpretation of reality, have found difficulty in facing the issues involved in this expansion of the world and of man's awareness of himself. Many people whose life and thought have been shaped and structured by Christianity bear inwardly the agonizing question: Is the Jesus of that now distant Mediterranean world still capable of embracing significantly the world of today? Can he remain the meaningful centre of our exploding universe? Will our cosmic expansion not shatter Christianity and eclipse God?

In the writings of Christian scholars the problem of man's relation to the physical world is widely acknowledged, but seldom defined. Cognizance is taken of the fact that "never before has it been so essential that we have an understanding of the interrelatedness of all living things," but in spite of these formal affirmations of the importance of our physical environment, indeed of its necessity for our understanding of God,[4] relatively little work has appeared

[4] "The knowledge of God which we have on earth is of a kind that

12

concerning the religious meaning of the earth and its lively role in our destiny. The antitheses of former ages have left so deep an imprint on our minds that the biblical significance of the material world has been obscured. The superiority of spirit over matter was deemed so great that we envisaged the community of man as our religious ideal, but in order to emphasise it, allowed the concept of the natural to fall into discredit. In the interests of "spiritual" religion the world was regarded as an enemy. In Protestantism everything human and natural sank into the night of sin, and languished there beyond hope of any discriminating judgement, in order that grace as God's unmerited favour might not be diminished. That the *unnatural* might be antithetical to the natural went unrecognised, and both were equally damned before the Word of God. The concept of the natural must therefore be reinstated. It must be shown that the very Word in whose presence the physical world was degraded is actually the Word that defines the essence of matter and validates its character.

We ourselves are not merely members of the human community, but also elements in the natural world; therefore the dualism which separates man's destiny from that of the world must be accounted dangerous. Inasmuch as all human life is deeply involved in the earth itself, man's regard for his physical environment and his consequent behaviour within it are of the highest importance for his well-being. Any attempt to establish human dignity that involves the degradation of the earth must bring about man's own

---

we cannot conceive to exist apart from some knowledge of things." John Baillie, *Our Knowledge of God* (London: Oxford University Press, 1939), p. 179.

undoing. Not only Carlyle's world as "one huge, dead, immeasurable steam-engine," but also the attitude held by many religious people, which regards the world as a stage upon which the drama of life is enacted, lead ultimately to the exploitation of the earth.

Michelangelo's drawings, it is said, constituted the discovery

of a single order, the machine, in man and in the world. Their delight is that the muscle and the joint are of a piece with the rope and the pulley.[5]

The world as a universal machine is a myth of modern man, who aims to elevate his personality to a point from which he may master the machine. But there cannot be a blundering or insensitive subjugation of the earth, not even in the name of the ideal of personality; for things are not so easily deprived of their power. A relationship which seeks to subject things to men reveals also the power of things over mankind. When we regard the world as a machine serving our purposes, we have to adapt ourselves to the ways of the machine. A mechanised world draws us into itself; we become cogs driven by the mechanical necessities we have created, and the attempt to elevate ourselves at the expense of nature brings a corresponding subordinateness in face of our own creations.

Much consideration is being given to relationships of Christianity to science and technology, and the present inquiry must take account of these, but its principal concern lies elsewhere. As far as human experiencing is con-

___

[5] J. Bronowski, *A Man without a Mask: William Blake* (London: Secker and Warburg, 1943), pp. 5–6.

cerned there are no things-in-themselves. What might be called "unconditioned" cannot be known by us; if it could, then it would not be unconditioned; so that knowing means placing oneself in relation with something, feeling oneself conditioned by something and oneself conditioning it. If, therefore, we evaluate science and technology from this understanding of what it means to know anything, then neither discipline is speaking merely about things or about the world. Each is expressing a particular relation of man to things. If science, for example, attempts to order into unity more and more phenomena, it is the experience of scientists themselves which is being reduced to a unity; so that to order the objective world is simultaneously to order the subjective.

Interpreting the inspiration of their predecessor Paul Cézanne, the painters Henri Matisse and Georges Braque speak of the reality of their art in terms of the relationship between observer and observed. In looking at nature Matisse is careful to include the observation of himself, and the discovery of a correspondence between himself and the exterior world. Braque endorses this viewpoint in the confession of his preference for being in unison with nature rather than for copying it. He does not paint a jug with the intention of making a utensil capable of holding water. Objects are the artist's poetics, and are therefore recreated for the purpose of playing their part in a picture. Thus the work of these painters concerns acts of seeing and of finding forms for those ideas and sensations which occur within the relationship. Nature does not present us with something absolutely fixed or unambiguous. Objects may be recreated to take their place in new configurations within the artist's

15

vision; and representational painting does not exclude this creative interplay between the painter and the rest of his universe.

Sir James Jeans is equally clear about the nature of scientific relationships with the world, and indicates that

complete objectivity can only be regained by treating observer and observed as parts of a single system; these must now be supposed to constitute an indivisible whole, which we must now identify with nature, the object of our studies. It now appears that this does not consist of something we perceive, but of our perceptions; it is not the object of the subject/object relation, but the relation itself.[6]

The question of which this thesis primarily treats, therefore, is not, What is the attitude of the Christian towards those particular, human relationships with the natural world described by the sciences, and expressed by technology?[7] but, What is the relation of the Christian man to the natural world itself?

In earlier times champions of the Christian religion earned notoriety for their spirited defiance of scientific views. Martin Luther described Copernicus as a new astrologer who wanted to prove "that the earth is moved and goeth around and not the Sky"; this view, he thought, was "the over-witty notion of a Fool, who would fain turn topsy-turvy the whole Art of Astronomy."[8] Bishop Wilberforce

[6] *Philosophy and Physics* (Cambridge: Cambridge University Press, 1943), p. 143.

[7] Michael Polanyi, *Personal Knowledge* (Chicago: University of Chicago Press, 1958), p. 178. The author characterises science and technology as follows: ". . . in science originality lies in the power of seeing more deeply than others into the nature of things, while in technology it consists in the ingenuity of the artificer in turning known facts to a surprising advantage."

[8] Quoted by Karl Heim, *Christian Faith and Natural Science* (London: SCM Press, 1953), p. 13.

16

pronounced the principle of natural selection to be incompatible with the Bible, and described evolution as an attempt to dethrone God. But these head-on collisions between religion and science no longer take place. Although the natural world seems to be a point at which religious evaluations and scientific disciplines might discover possibilities of conversation, man's curiosity about the earth appears to have been delegated largely to scientists. Although, as we noted, art is consciously open to the expression of a creative relationship between the painter and his world, this latter element seems often in recent decades to have been excluded from the equation, creating the impression that artists are bent upon freeing themselves from practical concepts and from the trammels of the external world. Theology, too, has concerned itself with man as a spiritual being to the exclusion of interest in his roots in the earth; its absorption with "history" has permitted it to assume the theological irrelevance of nature. A scientist complains that theologians speak as though only that area of life is significant which is portrayed by novelists, dramatists and artists —people, he suggests, who have not yet really discovered science; and he asks whether theology can continue to disregard scientific relationships with nature, which not only express certain attributes of man, but also shape his destiny.[9]

Surely, the fruits of man's scientific and technological relations with the world and its energies have now become matters which arouse concern as well as curiosity, and whose functions are clothed with anxiety; and well-founded criticism is directed against the effects of these disciplines

[9] H. K. Schilling, "A Contemporary Macedonian Plea," *Union Seminary Quarterly Review*, XVIII (January, 1963), pp. 113–33.

17

upon the personal aspects of man's life. Edmund Husserl goes so far as to suggest the possible mass rejection of science on account of its apparent indifference to human values.[10] For in spite of the fact that modern scientific enquiry is conducted mostly through communal enterprises, the personal values thus embedded in research can often be unquestioningly assumed. The conviction is growing, however, that mechanical and organic concepts of life must be integrated in a larger awareness of man's nature and potentialities as a person, that scientific and technological categories have to be incorporated in a synthesis which understands and does justice to man as a whole, and that within scientific activity itself an interpretative function must be born in order that science may grapple with its own meaning in relation to the rest of mankind.

A pope is quoted as saying: "Material comes out of the factory ennobled, the workers come out of it debased." Much technical research, for example, will probably consider the profits of those who finance it (and therefore the interests of consumers), before it takes account of the lives of those who operate machinery and maintain the processes of production.

Criticism of scientists, particularly of nuclear physicists, is no doubt stimulated by fear of the indiscriminate destruction of mankind, and added to this (in the case of criticism by religious persons) is the fact that the habit of scientific

---

[10] *Gesammelte Werke,* VI: *Die Krisis der europäischen Wissenschaften und die transzendentale Phänomenologie* (The Hague: Martinus Nijhoff, 1954) p. 4. *"In unserer Lebensnot—so hören wir—hat diese Wissenschaft uns nichts zu sagen. Gerade die Fragen schliesst sie prinzipiell aus, die für den in unseren unseligen Zeiten den schicksalsvollsten Umwälzungen preisgegebenen Menschen die brennenden sind: die Fragen nach Sinn oder Sinnlosigkeit dieses ganzen menschlichen Daseins."*

enquiry has tended to undermine the pursuit of religious faith.

Hitherto, the important themes of the Christian religion and its theological enquiry have been considered to be sin and redemption, grace and sacraments, faith and order: matters understood as relating to the salvation of man's soul. Beyond churchly frontiers men are concerned with questions of knowledge and survival; with categories of thought: time, space, substance and causality; with matter and energy; with the earth and its meaning; with scientific and technological changes that, consciously or unconsciously, fashion our destinies. The different concerns revealed by these two types of enquiry conceal presuppositions about the natural world which appear to be mutually opposed. The essence of the nonreligious enquiry is that it does not regard the natural world as hiding another world, or as veiling deeper realities lying beyond it; and those who adopt this view assume that the world of sensory experience is real in itself, and that there is no need to endow it with meaning derived from the appeal to another world or to realities "behind the scenes." This attitude alone must make natural theology of great significance.

Christianity is often criticised for its failure to communicate inspiration on account of its use of mythological language. A truer appraisal of man's so-called estrangement from religion might indicate that his estimate of the world itself has robbed much religious terminology and imagery of its meaning, and that references to "another world" cannot possibly refer to anything in his kind of universe. And if it comes to be shown that the stuff of the universe is not dead and mechanical, but contains the possibility of giving rise to the mind of man, to self-consciousness and love, then the Christianity of the future will be obliged to view the "material" world in a new light in order to capture man's allegiance. It will be obliged to enunciate a theology of the "inorganic" if it is to judge scientific and technological interpretations of the world and set them within a gospel for the total man. Simone Weil asks whether, if God loves man through men, he does not also love creation through them. And if creation suffers on man's account, she asks, does it not also need human love?

Friedrich Nietzsche, who frequently comes under formal attack from Christian pulpits, did Christianity much unrecognised service in his terrifying examination of the soul of modern man. His strong denials of God may have succeeded over wide areas of mankind in dethroning the God of "Christian morality," but at the same time they brought into focus the creative processes of the world. In Nietzsche's estimate the basic character of the entire universe is the Will to Power which "defines, determines gradations, differences of power" [11] and is nothing less than a creative intelligence. And this evaluating, interpretative faculty with which Nietzsche endowed the Will to Power forced him occasionally to recognise that his attack upon Christendom had not entirely abolished the God who creates and sustains the world and when divested of his "moral integument" manages to reappear beyond good and evil.

Since Nietzsche pointed with great force and conviction to the earth and its creative energies, others have reflected his insights. Christian thinkers, therefore, preoccupied with what they consider to be of prime importance, but who neglect or set aside the teaching of the Logos in respect of

[11] *The Complete Works of Friedrich Nietzsche,* ed. Oscar Levy (New York: Russell & Russell, 1964); XV, *Will to Power,* pp. 124–25. All subsequent references to Nietzsche's writings will be to this edition.

creation, should not be surprised if others have emphasised libido rather than Logos in this context. If every existing thing is equally upheld in its existence by God's creative love, the friends of God are bound to love him to the point of merging their love in his with regard to all things; but this love is hard to kindle.

It may be impossible to explain completely the reluctance of Christian theology to speak about man's natural environment in terms other than those that underrate its significance. Biblical religion finds it impossible to deify the natural world; indeed, man's awareness of sin is reflected in his environment; nature suffers violence at men's hands, and becomes involved in man's derelictions. Yet the passionate ethical monotheism at the heart of Judaism and Christianity, unable to endure the thought that God is the author of evil, concluded that the evil which it discovered in man and in the world must be due to some spontaneous revolt against God, a voluntary aberration from the path marked out for man by his Creator, to a "fall" of some kind. And this teaching of the fall may have been deemed adequate to account for the discrepancy between the goodness of the Creator and the evil in the world, as well as expressing man's need for redemption. The doctrine of the fall may therefore have cushioned theological thinking against the harsh impact which faith must feel when the thought of the perfection of the Creator is set over against the fallen condition of his creation.

The inability or unpreparedness of Christianity to conceive of its relationship to matter [12] is poignantly evident in the diversity and confusion of views with which it regards

---

[12] The attitude and achievement of St. Francis of Assisi constitute an outstanding exception to this general obtuseness of Christianity with regard to matter, and will be noticed in Chap. 9.

21

the elements used in the sacrament of the Lord's Supper. These fragments of matter at the heart of Christianity have led to scandal and division among Christians, while attempted solutions of the mystery of the relationship seem largely to be sought in the direction of Christ and man. Might not an enquiry into the interrelatedness of man and his physical environment deepen and enliven the significance of the elements themselves and the part they play in the sacramental life of the Church?

William Temple's Gifford Lectures, *Nature, Man and God*, still challenge and press us towards the kind of enquiry visualised here. His now famous dictum states that

one ground for the hope of Christianity that it may make good its claim to be the true faith lies in the fact that it is the most avowedly materialist of all the great religions. It affords an expectation that it may be able to control that material, precisely because it does not ignore it or deny it, but roundly asserts alike the reality of matter and its subordination. Its own most central saying is: 'The Word was made flesh', where the last term was, no doubt, chosen because of its specially materialistic associations. By the very nature of its central doctrine Christianity is committed to a belief in the ultimate significance of the historical process, and in the reality of matter and its place in the divine scheme.[13]

Again, man's thinking is sometimes of the kind that rationalises his life in this world, and at other times it is of the sort which intuits the nature of things. The early Greek cosmologists were intuitive thinkers whose first proposition originated in a mystic intuition that in this world, "Everything is one." They took for granted a harmony between the

[13] *Nature, Man and God:* Gifford Lectures, 1932–34 (London: Macmillan, 1953), p. 478.

external and internal worlds, and held as true of the external that which corresponded with the internal. By correspondence they meant becoming aware of an experience of satisfaction in their relationship with the world.

This kind of thinking may popularly be considered to belong only to poets. Baudelaire says: *"La première condition nécessaire pour faire un art sain est la croyance à l'unité intégrale."* But this faith is also ensconced in the heart of scientific thinking where creative imagination itself stretches uncertain fingers towards new light and understanding. Sir Edward Appleton, the British physicist, reiterates the myth of the early cosmologists:

So I want to make the assumption which the astronomer—and indeed any scientist—makes about the universe he investigates. It is this: that the same physical cause gives rise to the same physical results anywhere in the universe, and at any time, past, present and future. The fuller examination of this basic assumption, and much else besides, belongs to philosophy. The scientist, for his part, makes the assumption I have mentioned as an act of faith; and he feels confirmed in that faith by his increasing ability to build up a consistent and satisfying picture of the universe and its behaviour.[14]

Man's scientific relationship with the world springs out of the myth of its unity. The Bible, too, reveals a similar mythological strand which guides its readers towards an immense concept of cosmic reconciliation, a quality of atonement which embraces the scientific myth of the oneness of the world and a personal dimension, and visualises man reconciled within his total environment.

Religious views of the world often rest upon the belief that man distinguishes himself in worth from all the phe-

[14] *Science and the Nation: BBC Reith Lectures for 1956* (Edinburgh: Edinburgh University Press, 1957), p. 49.

23

nomena around him and seeks by means of spiritual powers which he reverences, a solution to the contradiction in which he finds himself as part of nature and as a spiritual personality claiming to dominate nature.[15]

The present thesis is not an attempt to solve this contradiction, but takes issue with the idea of "dominating" nature, and suggests that on account of the liveliness of the universe and man's essential relationship with it, "to dominate" must simultaneously mean "to be dominated by." A relationship to nature less aggressive than that which now prevails, characterised by a "lordliness" of humility must be of the greatest importance to mankind. Of this relationship the thesis asks, Is it possible? and, What steps may we take towards it?

In the light of man's thinking about the earth and his behavior upon it, the Hebrew-Christian Scriptures may also conceivably be read with new eyes, enabling us to behold there those "sons of God" for whom creation waits: men not simply careful of their relations with each other, but who cultivate a responsible bearing towards their natural environment; men of ecological conscience as well as social conscience, knowing themselves and their destiny bound up with the earth.

Kierkegaard's classic description of the "knight of faith," a man of secular sanctity, is regarded as singularly lacking in love for his neighbours, and it is suggested that this

[15] Cf. Albrecht Ritschl, *The Christian Doctrine of Justification and Reconciliation* (Edinburgh: T. & T. Clark, 1902), p. 279: "Nature, therefore, must likewise be explained from the Divine Will in its self-given character of love. But, owing to its lack of kinship with God, it cannot be the direct object and the last end of His loving will. And so nothing remains but to conclude, that nature is called into being to serve as a means to God's essential purpose in creating the world of spirits."

omission reflects Kierkegaard's own personal failure to realise "the universal human." The picture clearly expresses, however, Christ's reconciling grace in the knight's relation to the world of nature and to the objects about him.

The knight of faith . . . belongs entirely to the world. . . . He takes delight in everything, and whenever one sees him taking part in a particular pleasure, he does it with the persistence which is the mark of the earthly man whose soul is absorbed in such things. . . . He takes delight in everything he sees, in the human swarm, in the new omnibuses, in the waters of the Sound; . . . he is interested in everything that goes on, in a rat which slips under the curb, in the children's play.[16]

The "knight" is evidently a man for whom the things of this world are really interesting in themselves, in whose mind the "truth of things" is not engulfed and lost in some higher reference, and whose search for an *elsewhere* has led to the discovery that elsewhere is essentially *here*.

That some of the intellectual objections to Christianity at the present time receive unconvincing replies is due to the absence of a generally accepted natural theology. This circumstance reflects the fact that outside Catholic traditions natural theology has been widely neglected and spurned. If we no longer adhere to the view of revelation as divinely imparted knowledge of God in propositional form, but account that God reveals himself in the human needs and conditions by which our understanding is also stimulated, then it seems impossible to abstract the world from the processes of our understanding of God. If creation can say nothing to us of God, despite our inextricable part in it, we

---

[16] Kierkegaard, *Fear and Trembling,* trans. Walter Lowrie (Princeton: Princeton University Press, 1941), pp. 52 ff.

cannot suppose that deductions from Scripture will be without flaw, unless we believe the transmission of divine revelation through literal Scripture to be mechanically unimpaired! If Christianity sheds light upon the natural world, then the reflections it receives back must affect its own shape and appearance; but the following exploration of man in his environment does not examine the effect of this relationship upon Christian doctrine except where the common destiny of man and matter demands that notice be taken of teaching about immortality and resurrection.

The exercise of brinkmanship may include the question, How far dare man remove himself from nature and not be overcome or destroyed by it? When Christianity reflects its sources it scans another horizon to behold a world waiting, though not passively, for man's recognition of its rightful place in his destiny.

1

The Significance of Variety

We individual men and women are not merely members of the human community but elements of the natural world. We have in the end to face the question of our relation to the world. How is it to be conceived? How must we represent the world and the relation between ourselves and the world?

John Macmurray [1]

> *Since man has been articulate*
> *Mechanical, improvidently wise*
> *(Servant of Fate),*
> *He has not understood the little cries*
> *And foreign conversations of the small*
> *Delightful creatures that have followed him*
> *Not far behind;*
> *Has failed to hear the sympathetic call*
> *Of Crockery and Cutlery, those kind*
> *Reposeful Teraphim*
> *Of his domestic happiness; the Stool*
> *He sat on, or the Door he entered through:*
> *He has not thanked them, overbearing fool!*
> *What is he coming to?*

Harold Monro [2]

AUTOBIOGRAPHICAL WRITING long ago revealed that explorers and shipwrecked mariners who undergo isolation for many days may suffer curious mental abnormalities. In recent years it has been found that prisoners-of-war exposed to brain-washing have sometimes experienced similar dis-

[1] *Persons in Relation: Gifford Lectures,* 1954 (London: Faber and Faber, 1961), p. 212.

[2] Quoted from "Every Thing," in *Collected Poems* (London: Cobden-

27

turbances, which are not due entirely to loneliness or the absence of other human beings, as might easily be supposed, but have been shown to be partly the products of a monotony of environment.

In the hullabaloo of modern life thinking people are occasionally driven to ponder whither they are being carried—and long for some quiet place in which to reason undisturbed—and to take stock of themselves. Admiral Byrd was such a person who, wishing to be by himself for a while and "to taste peace and quiet and solitude long enough to find out how good they really are," [3] spent six months alone in the Antarctic. Byrd believed that any intelligent man should be able to find the means of existence within himself. He practised his preachments of a disciplined mind, and focussed his thinking upon healthy, constructive images and concepts in order to crowd out the unhealthy ones:

I built a wall between myself and the past in an effort to extract every ounce of diversion and creativeness inherent in my immediate surroundings. Every day I experimented with new schemes for increasing the content of the hours.[4]

Added to this Byrd cultivated an attitude of thankfulness for his environment, believing that "a grateful environment" can stimulate us from without as good works may stimulate us from within. He wished to be in full mastery of the impinging moment; and after three months, when depression settled upon him, still believing that the explanation of his dispeace lay within himself, he studied his mood, tried to locate the source of his inner conflicts in order to harmonise them, but was driven to a different conclusion. His attitude towards himself was surely a sensible one, yet it

Sanderson, 1933), pp. 119–20. Reprinted by permission of the Bodley Head Ltd.

[3] R. E. Byrd, *Alone* (London: G. Putnam & Sons, 1938), p. 4.

[4] *Ibid.*, pp. 132–33.

suffered from glibness and the failure to recognise that beyond the censorship and control of the mind lay also the concerns of the body and the outcry of the total person.

Subsequently, Byrd was obliged to write as follows:

I did not recognize . . . that the whole complex nervous-muscular mechanism which is the body was waiting, as if with bated breath, for the intrusion of familiar stimuli from the outside world, and could not comprehend why they were denied. A man can isolate himself from habits and conveniences . . . and force his mind to forget. But the body is not so easily side-tracked. It keeps on remembering. Habit has set up in the core of the being a system of automatic physio-chemical actions and reactions which insist upon replenishment. That is where the conflict arises. I don't think that a man can do without sounds and smells and voices and touch any more than he can do without phosphorus and calcium.[5]

The root of the problem lay in the poverty of the stimuli arising out of the environment: "This damnable *evenness* is getting me!" [6]

Another dedicated scientist, Dr. Alain Bombard, reacted in almost identical fashion to loneliness and isolation. He wished to prove that shipwrecked people could survive at sea for an indefinite period of time, and therefore sailed alone across the Atlantic for sixty-five days on a life raft, subsisting solely upon what he could obtain from the ocean.

Dr. Bombard used the same mechanism as did Admiral Byrd to fight off depression. He created a routine of work in order to remain master of events and as a defence against loneliness. He controlled his thoughts by dwelling upon the pleasant associations and experiences of the past, and refusing to allow himself to think about those aspects of his situ-

[5] *Ibid.,* p. 131.
[6] *Ibid.,* p. 243.

ation which might arouse anxiety. For emotional sustenance he drew deeply upon his inner personal resources, but the constancy of his surroundings, the unchanging changefulness of the ocean, gathered oppressively into a destructive force. Not only was his need for human company overwhelming, but

it seemed sometimes as if the immense and absolute solitude of the ocean's expanse was concentrated right on top of me, as if my beating heart was the centre of gravity of a mass which was at the same time nothingness. . . . It was a vast presence which engulfed me. Its spell could not be broken any more than the horizon could be brought nearer. And if from time to time I talked aloud in order to hear my own voice, I only felt more alone, a hostage to silence.[7]

Dr. Bombard found it frightening to realise to what extent one can develop a persecution mania alone on the surface of the sea.[8]

Although brain-washing, or thought control, has existed for centuries, it has taken on a new and sinister meaning in the contemporary world. To the older techniques of thought reform have been added subtler manipulations of the physical environment which assist in the transformation of a community of persons into a group of isolates, each man on his own life raft. Prisoners-of-war, for example, segregated according to rank, race and nationality, and indicted as war criminals so as to render meaningless the idea of belonging to a military unit, have their correspondence regulated and are separated from the support and companionship of others. Enforced solitary confinement almost completes the severance of social ties, but in addition to this it has been found that the impoverishment of

[7] A. Bombard, *The Bombard Story* (London: Deutsch, 1953), p. 144.
[8] *Ibid.*, p. 181.

their sensory life, exposure to a monotonous environment, completes both the disorganisation of their persons and the process of "dying in order to be reborn." A prisoner who experienced solitary confinement for eighteen months during the Second World War says:

I soon learned that variety is not the spice, but the very stuff of life. We need the constant ebb and flow of wavelets of sensation, thought, perception, action and emotion, lapping on the shore of our consciousness, now here, now there, keeping even our isolation in the ocean of reality, so that we neither encroach nor are encroached upon. . . . We are narrow men, twisted men, smooth and nicely rounded men, and poets; but whatever we are, we have our shape, and we perceive it best in the experience of many things.[9]

Although situations of this kind, with which explorers contended and which prisoners had thrust upon them, include the interaction of many factors, they seem to indicate that the stability of the mental state of human beings requires among other conditions a variety of perceptual contacts with the surrounding world.

With this evidence to suggest the need for continual sensory bombardment in order to maintain normal, intelligent and adaptive behaviour, it was natural to speculate about the effects of reduced sensory stimulation. Clearly, it is impossible to exclude completely all sensory experience from external sources and still maintain a responsible human being who is able to observe what is happening, but it has been possible by the use of ingenious devices and by rigid forms of confinement, to create conditions in which both the amount and the variety of sensory contacts are drastically reduced.

During the last decade experiments have been conducted

[9] Christopher Burney, *Solitary Confinement* (London: Clerke and Cockeran, 1952), p. 16.

31

which show the effects upon human beings of sensory deprivation.[10] Here, for example, is a brief indication of the method and results of an attempt to secure the most rigid conditions of isolation consistent with reasonable physical comfort.[11] A massively insulated cubicle, ventilated—yet so as to exclude all sounds from fan motors and air streams—and approached through a series of soundproof doors, was suspended in an already silent room. Temperature was controlled, and the people who volunteered to spend time in this small room could either rest on a comfortable bed or walk about to avoid the discomforts which may attend immobility. Their eyes were covered with translucent goggles which excluded patterned vision; hands and arms were enclosed in padded fur gauntlets; these and cotton gloves effectively reduced tactile sensation, while heavy woollen socks were pulled over their feet. Volunteers remained in the cubicle for as long as they could endure the conditions, and always knew that they could terminate the experiment at any time by telling the observer or by letting themselves out of the room. The completeness of their isolation was rendered partial only when they were given meals and briefly questioned four times a day.

Twenty volunteers underwent this experience: eleven men and nine women. All spent varying periods, between six and ninety-two hours, under these conditions of sensory deprivation. There were many individual reactions. Seven people suffered body-image disturbances, especially in relation to the head and arms: "My arm is like a ton weight and

[10] *The Lancet,* 12th December, 1959, in a leading article (pp. 1072–73) gives a list of research workers in this field and the sources at which descriptions of their experiments are to be found.

[11] *The Lancet,* 12th September, 1959, pp. 342–45.

feels fatter than my body." "My head is like a spinning cone going away from my body." But the chief difficulty was concentration. In many volunteers it was lost, and in two cases preceded the complete disorganisation of thought. In the majority of cases it was disordered thinking that produced the unbearable anxiety or panic attacks which terminated all twenty experiments, so that it was possible to observe a general sequence of events. The pattern was briefly this: increasing sleep was followed by restlessness and agitation which, in turn, was succeeded by thinking difficulties and culminating panic.

In a symposium discussing "Control of the Mind" [12] it was suggested that the spectacular symptoms displayed by test subjects in short-term deprivation experiments were obtained by influencing systematically the subjects' previous knowledge of the expected results of the test. For instance, subjects who knew beforehand that they were expected to have hallucinations, obliged by having them. This kind of response has probably been made in some instances. The influence of preconceived attitudes upon the outcome of the experiments in which the subject was not expected to react according to a pattern changed the meaning of the results, and experiments designed to show the effects of sensory deprivation have revealed instead the power of suggestion. But this criticism cannot invalidate the inferences drawn by the explorers and the prisoner whose experiences have been recounted in this chapter. They were confronted with phenomena attendant upon their privations without having anticipated any particular effects. They were naturally de-

[12] Organised by the University of California Medical Center, San Francisco, 1961. Reported by Arthur Koestler in *The Observer* (London), 23rd April, 1961.

termined to cope with life as it assailed them, and were prepared to confront it with patterns of personal discipline; but above all, they wished to remain normal, so that abnormal states of being, under conditions of solitude and monotony, were not positively anticipated by them. And they had no mentors whom they would have been reluctant to disappoint.

This close relation between man and his physical environment is not, of course, a recent development in human awareness, but it does make a renewed impact upon that attitude of mind, common in our generation, which regards the created world as the stage—together with its properties —upon which the drama of our existence unfolds. Mediaeval philosophers held the view that the whole material creation existed for the sake of man, whose intellectual being had to be manufactured, so to speak, out of the data supplied to the mind by the material world through the senses. In addition to supplying the actual tissues and organs of man's body, the Schoolmen held that the material universe does man a threefold service:

It sustains the body that it has formed, it feeds the mind and enables it to set its own processes to work and educate and develop itself; and it provides an instrument for self-expression in the practical and fine arts.[13]

In modern times, against the assumption that the world is being run for our benefit, is set an unmistakeable question mark, and a great deal of spiritual and intellectual exercise is being performed both to ascertain and to create truer relationships between human beings and their physical surroundings.

In reply to the question as to whether or not conscious-

[13] P. H. Wicksteed, *The Reactions between Dogma and Philosophy* (London: Constable, 1926), p. 370.

ness exists, William James denied that the word stood for an entity, but insisted emphatically that it did stand for the function of knowing.

'Consciousness' is supposed necessary to explain the fact that things not only are, but get reported, are known. Whoever blots out the notion of consciousness from his list of first principles must still provide in some way for that function's being carried on.[14]

He argues here that consciousness (*con-scientia*) describes the relationships which exist between our minds, our bodies and the external world; that it stands for the multitudinous and infinitely variable processes which have in common the experience of our being aware of something; that consciousness is a term which we abstract from life, while life itself is characterised rather by *consciousness of something*.[15]

It is often loosely asserted that physical environment influences our persons. Indeed, our dependence upon the world of creatures and things requires no argument. Were we not already aware of the tragic mental and physical symptoms accompanying starvation among multitudes of the world's people, then the protestations of an empty stomach might themselves be sufficiently eloquent! Not only are we nourished by the earth, but to an extent far greater than has been generally realised, the sanity and balance of our persons is maintained by the constant but varying stimuli of the external world and our sensory experience of them.

In quite recent years neurologists have been able to de-

[14] *Essays on Radical Empiricism* (New York: Longmans, Green, 1912), p. 4.

[15] Cf. *Brain Mechanisms and Consciousness: A Symposium,* ed. J. F. Delafresnaye (Oxford: Blackwell, 1954), contribution by L. S. Kubie, pp. 446 f.

scribe what happens when an object is perceived. A series of events occurs successively in time, beginning with an event in the object, and ending with an event in the subject's brain. Sir W. Russell Brain speaks about the pathways by which sensory impulses travel within the nervous system, showing that although we discriminate between sights, sounds and smells, the events in the nervous system by which these varying stimuli are translated into sensation differ only in that the nervous impulses which transmit them travel by different paths and reach different destinations in the brain.[16]

Sense data as we perceive them, it seems, are not transmitted by the external world but engendered by the brain itself, which has a highly developed capacity for reproducing the structure of things around us, and these sensory qualities which the brain produces may be regarded as symbolical representations of the properties of objects.

The same neurologist has elsewhere illustrated this relationship between our seeing and the external world by analogy with a ship's radar. He asks us to imagine ourselves on board ship sailing through the night off a rocky coast. All that is visible is the radar image of the ship's environment. The mountainous hinterland is depicted in yellowish luminosity on the screen. The picture changes as the journey proceeds, and ahead an approaching vessel appears.

The radar contributes its own sense data in the form of luminous images which reproduce the structure of the environment otherwise unperceived by us; and the images are sufficient to enable the captain to steer his vessel with safety. In looking at the ship's radar, we recognise that we

[16] W. Russell Brain, *Mind, Perception and Science* (Oxford: Blackwell, 1951), p. 4.

are not merely seeing a relatively small picture, but viewing, simultaneously, the external world. Through the private space-time of the apparatus we become aware of a physical space-time in which the ship, the land and the sea itself exist.[17]

This thesis that we know concrete material things by the medium of their complements within ourselves has been advanced by scholars pursuing a variety of disciplines. In earlier times Dionysius the Areopagite and St. Thomas Aquinas used the term "connaturality" to describe the ability to understand the human qualities in other people by virtue of the fact that we share in them ourselves. There is a creatureliness about us which extends the scope of connaturality far into the realm of nature, but with the rise of science in our civilisation this particular relationship to the natural world has been gradually limited to artistic and poetic experience:

> The mind, that Ocean where each kind
> Does straight its own resemblance find.[18]

To this particular aspect of the relationship between man and things we shall return. This chapter has sought simply to establish the "inseparability of mind and externality." In the Gifford Lectures of 1911 Bernard Bosanquet says that nature is complementary to mind and continuous with it: "You cannot say where self ends and environment begins." [19] In his view the complementarity of man and

[17] W. Russell Brain, *The Nature of Experience*, Durham University, Riddell Memorial Lectures, 30th Series, 1958 (London: Oxford University Press, 1959), p. 41.

[18] From Andrew Marvell, "Thoughts in a Garden" in *The Oxford Book of English Verse* (Oxford: Clarendon Press, 1939), p. 402.

[19] *The Principle of Individuality and Value* (London: Macmillan, 1912), pp. 358–62.

37

things is the condition in which both the content of the universe may be known by us, and the proposition allowed that "nature is in some sense plastic and responsive to finite subjective mind."

Sir Charles Sherrington illustrates the relationship as follows:

Our own seeing makes so rich a contribution to the shapes of our world that it is a little puzzling for us to think of unpatterned seeing . . . over a diversity of more highly developed vision, the eye supplies a definite image of what it looks at.[20]

We can have no knowledge of the external world except insofar as it confronts us and affects us inwardly; yet it is always through and by something within ourselves that we know it. Awareness is always awareness of something; and within this mutuality the responsiveness of nature is not unmatched; human awareness is itself modified, and in such a way that some of the characteristics of our surroundings become part of our consciousness. But more than this: the external element of our interdependent life-in-this-world, the sensory bombardment of the human being from environmental sources, cannot be heedlessly impaired or interrupted beyond certain limits without the disorganisation and derangement of the living person. It is impossible to abstract human personality from the living environment of things; the attempt to isolate it by depriving human beings of the sensory experience, which begins in events outside, must end in the destruction of personality as we know it. We are literally obliged to speak of the inseparability of man from things!

[20] *Man on His Nature* (London: Pelican, 1955) p. 117.

2

Body and Soul

Let us not always say
'Spite of this flesh to-day
I strove, made head, gained ground upon the whole.'
As the bird wings and sings,
Let us cry 'All good things
Are ours, nor soul helps flesh
More than flesh helps soul.'

Robert Browning [1]

Mind knows the world and operates on the world by means of
its body. It is hard to escape the conclusion that bodies existed
before minds and minds only exist because there are bodies fit
for them.

A. D. Ritchie [2]

OUR THINKING ABOUT MAN and his physical environment
cannot avoid those frontier zones which exist sometimes in
the realm of self-awareness, and extend at other times into
the world outside. The growth of human beings to maturity
is marked by a recognition of nonbodily factors, but at no
point in our development does the body become unes-
sential. The noblest aspirations, the highest flights of fancy
and intelligence, the most heroic decisions spring to life "in
the flesh." Our human actuality is both material and immaterial, and is therefore described in dualistic terms.

From classical times to the present day philosophers have

[1] *"Rabbi ben Ezra,"* xii, *Complete Poetic and Dramatic Works of Rob-*
ert Browning (Boston and New York: Houghton-Mifflin, 1895), p. 384.
[2] *Natural History of Mind* (London: Longmans, Green, 1936), pp.
9–10.

frequently equated the self-as-subject with mind, and the self-as-object with body; and for purposes of analysis this theoretical dividing of human beings has proved both necessary and valuable. But human beings are not *actually* divisible in this way. The term "split personality" is used to represent a pathological condition of the mind, and the word "individual" refers to the indivisible one, the undivided self.

Man's understanding of himself is also reflected in his view of the world. In remote antiquity, perhaps from experiences of dreaming and fainting, of ecstasy and possession, men deduced a distinction between body and soul, and came to recognise that the world itself was neither simply physical nor simply mental, but that each experience required its physical datum and its mental reaction to bring it to actuality. Between Plato's "souls" and "physical" nature, between the thinking and extended substances of Descartes, between the human understanding and external things of John Locke, there exists a dualism within each occasion of actuality. These explanations of experience, however, do not represent an ultimate dualism, but point rather towards that unity of opposites which is their ground. The misfortunes of our century may tempt some despairing people to believe that an ultimate dualism is a correct explanation of the universe, but few philosophers have held to such a creed, and even during the darkest times dualism has never been widely accepted.

Belief in an ultimate dualism of body and soul is often ascribed to the Greeks, but closer acquaintance with their literature hardly confirms this view. Homer may stress the supremacy of the body and Plato that of the soul—but for both, the world is one. In the Homeric poems human activities are possible only so long as body and soul are together, and in the strictest sense human activities are bodily functions, while mental attitudes and faculties express physical power and do not spring from any inherent capacity of the soul as such. For Homer, the soul is an ineffective shadow, while even the lifeless body is repeatedly spoken of as the true self (αὐτός) and set in contrast with the psyche.[3]

In contrast to this Homeric understanding of personality Plato cherishes the soul which God made superior to the body in origin, excellence and authority. "The soul in her totality has the care of inanimate being everywhere." [4] The disengagement of the soul from the world of sense and appearance is its proper goal, its sojourn in the body clouds its happiness and knowledge till it returns to the place and condition of its heavenly origin, there to be gladdened and replenished in beholding reality.

These dualistic forms must not, however, be taken to imply an ultimate dualism. For Plato the world is primarily one:

Are we right in saying that there is one world . . . ? There must be one only. The creator made not two worlds or an infinite number of them; but there is and ever will be one.[5]

Popularised Platonism often takes a dualistic form, but neither in Plato nor in Plotinus is there any justification for the notion that there are two world principles and two worlds.[6]

In contrast to these emphases of Homer and Plato, Aristotle formulates an organic view of the relationship

[3] Cf. "Body," by W. Capelle, in *Encyclopaedia of Religion and Ethics*, II, ed. James Hastings (New York: Scribners, 1908–22), p. 279.

[4] *Phaedrus*, in *The Dialogues of Plato*, I, trans. B. Jowett (3rd ed.; New York: Oxford University Press, 1892), p. 452.

[5] *Timaeus*, in *Dialogues of Plato*, op. cit., III, p. 450.

[6] "Neo-Platonism" by W. R. Inge, in *Encyclopaedia of Religion and Ethics*, IX, p. 309.

41

between soul and body. Nature's processes move without break in an ascending scale from the inanimate world to the most intricate forms of animate existence. Bodily and mental developments belong to one continuous process. The soul is the entelechy of the body: that is to say, when the potentialities of the body become actual, *that* is soul.[7] Body and soul in a living person may well be distinguished as concepts, but cannot be dissociated in actuality, for the soul is the natural realisation of the body. Aristotle describes the closeness of this relationship by saying that if the body were an eye, seeing would be its soul. According to his dominant mood, therefore, a discarnate soul is a contradiction in terms.

Each of these three estimates of the body-soul complex has representatives to give it credence in modern times, but our expanding knowledge of the world and of the nature of matter, our questions concerning the frontier at which "dead" matter ceases and organic life begins, the manifestation of wisdom and of powers of choice in forms of life hitherto regarded as lifeless objects, seem to point to Aristotle's view as that which contained the highest possibility of future development.

The briefest description of man's immediate awareness of himself reveals the labyrinthine complexity of the soul. Sense perceptions are limited to what is present in time and space, but on the basis of these data imagination creates images of what is remotely past or distantly future or even nonexistent from the point of view of the senses. Imagination, nourished by sense impressions, so transposes them as to produce results within its own "imaginary" space and time, which is not that of the external world.

[7] Aristotle, *On the Soul,* trans. by W. S. Hett (Cambridge, Mass.: Harvard University Press, 1957), p. 80.

These capacities for transcending ordinary time and space intermingle with the steady internal dialogue that proceeds upon various levels of the soul. Human beings are probably the only creatures who talk to themselves, and in this converse one aspect of the self may make another aspect the object of its attention. We may and do become spectators of our own thoughts and actions. We transcend ourselves, and it is this capacity which gives us the ability to judge our own actions and attitudes, and makes possible the tension between duty and desire, between obligation and inclination, which we call conscience. "Morality," explains C. G. Jung, "is a function of the human soul. It is not imposed from outside; we have it in ourselves from the start." [8] The statement that conscience is relative to the environment in which it develops is limited by the frequency with which conscience expresses itself in defiance of its environment.

This freedom of the soul to rise above its functions, to confirm or deny the wisdom of the body, to lord it over reason so that reason justifies even the most exorbitant desires is not easily obscured in the broader reaches of human experience. Despite the determining influences of social pressure and personal inhibition, this self-determination of the soul, though empirically indefinable, is widely assumed to be real. Psychiatry requires the voluntary co-operation of the patient and confesses to the futility of forced submission to therapy. Jurisprudence invariably assumes a responsible freedom of the self, though law may recognise "insanity" as limiting responsibility. And what becomes of the tragic hero when man's capacity for self-determination ceases?

[8] *Two Essays on Analytical Psychology,* in *Collected Works,* VII, trans. by R. F. C. Hull (London: Routledge & Kegan Paul, 1953), p. 26.

Scientifically regarded this freedom of the soul may be "illusory," for it is not distinct from its organism—the body; nor can it be dissociated from its perceptual responses—the mind; yet it is not to be equated with body or mind, or even with both together. It contributes to the dialogue within itself; it is aware of a freedom over its functions, but it is also accompanied by a sense of its unity with the whole. And this ability of the soul to stand above its functions and capacities, to be related to its inner divisions and yet to have freedom over them, is what has often been called "spirit."

But the territories of the soul extend beyond these limits. This partial account of our self-awareness might be summarised by Socrates in the *Phaedo* as "the habit of the soul gathering and collecting herself into herself from all sides of the body; the dwelling in her own place alone, as in another life." But the realm of conscious life expands in an interior direction with every incursion into the Unconscious. Our present purpose is to explore the extensive qualities of the soul, to observe its penetration into the world of things, so that we may only stand for a moment in wonder upon the threshold of this mysterious, unfathomed dimension of man's inwardness. Pierre Teilhard de Chardin captures this awesome moment in *Le milieu divin:*

I took the lamp and, leaving the zone of everyday occupations and relationships where everything seems clear, I went down into my inmost self, to the deep abyss whence I feel dimly that life is superficially illuminated, I became aware that I was losing my power of action emanates. But as I moved further and further away from the conventional certainties by which social contact with myself. At each step of the descent a new person was disclosed within me of whose name I was no longer sure, and who no longer obeyed me. And when I had to stop my

44

exploration because the path faded from beneath my steps, I found a bottomless abyss at my feet, and out of it came—arising I know not from where—the current which I dare to call *my* life.[9]

And so, with this terrifying glimpse of hidden resources and conflicts, we look across another "frontier" of the soul into the world outside.

Within the kingdom of the soul all the occasions of our experience are allowed to gather at two opposite poles which we call "I myself" and "the external world," and the concept of the body either vacillates or is made to pass to and fro between these poles. Sometimes a thought is fathered upon the world outside when, for example, we say, "That was not I; an evil thought took possession of me." With greater frequency, however, we dissociate our bodies from our selves and make them participate in the external world. We can withdraw from part of the body and may say, "This is not I; it is only my finger."

Our capacity for self-transcendence allows us to sense ourselves as a kind of inner personality, lodging telescoped within a more superficial personality, the body; and we may see ourselves both as the most imaginary and as the most positive beings. Here, then, are two aspects of the soul: one which includes my body and ranges itself over against the external world; and another in which I have retreated inwardly from my body, leaving it to participate in the world "outside."

In their desire to apprehend the universe as a systematic whole men have attempted to resolve the apparent dichotomy between "I myself" and "the external world" by reasoning from one pole or the other. Beginning with "I my-

[9] Trans. Bernard Wall (London: Collins, 1960), pp. 54–55.

self" they have argued that all experience occurs within us; that part of our experience which seems to have an independent existence as the external world is simply inward experience projected outwards. This is solipsism. Beginning with "the external world" others have argued that the soul is nothing more than a function of the body, the organs of sense and the brain, so that "I myself" am a product of sense impressions. This is materialism.

To treat of either pole as absolute and capable of absorbing its opposite, which then vanishes, leads to one or other of these extreme conclusions. It is the polarity in our awareness which constitutes concrete being. On this account Thomas Aquinas strikes a modern note by asserting that body and soul are an immediate existential unity, and that the ultimate bearer of our knowledge is not mind or "spirit" but man composed of body and soul.[10]

The two aspects of the soul, in the first of which the total person was set over against the world outside, and in the second the soul withdrew from the whole or part of the body leaving it to participate in the external world, indicate that the body occupies a frontier zone. "I myself" and "the external world" are not sharply delimited. At one moment what I call "my body" is being apprehended as the object of my sensory perceptions; in the next moment, equally justifiably, it is the active subject, the indispensable basis of "I myself," apprehending experience, the sole sentient representation of "me." [11]

But the moment we focus attention upon one member of

[10] *Summa theologica*, I, 75, 4.

[11] This and some later paragraphs owe much to an early chapter in Ernst Kretschmer, *A Textbook of Medical Psychology*, trans. E. B. Strauss (London: Hogarth, 1952).

the body to the exclusion of the others, that member no longer participates consciously in the nature of "me"; we begin to regard it as a kind of possession. It is "my hand" or "my leg" in much the same way that we say "my glove" or "my shoe"; it is only "me" when we regard it within the totality of our persons. And those members of the body not linked to it by virtue of sensory or motor functions, such as the ends of the hair and nails, are always losing their identity with "me," and are ever passing over in the direction of "the external world." They occupy a transitional zone in company with things which have crossed the same border country, but in an opposite direction, and now find themselves in close proximity to the body. Clothing, for example, moves in this direction. We normally understand clothes to be external to ourselves, but they enjoy a small measure of our self-awareness and become an extended part of us when we say, "You touched me," when only our clothing was touched. Such an awareness may account for the action of the woman in the Gospel and the response of Jesus, whose garment she touched (Matt. 9:20–22). There is a valid sense in which the soul extends into its immediate spatial surroundings, but in relation to clothing the word "soul" may popularly be replaced by the term "personality."

Once we have crossed the periphery of the body we may go on to notice our use of instruments as extensions of our hands, our senses and our intelligence. We assimilate tools and instruments to our bodies and minds by pouring ourselves into them, and whenever we thus assimilate a tool or an instrument to our persons, our identity undergoes some change and we expand into new modes of being. Indeed, man's penetration into nature, which often raises the fear of

47

what is called his "dehumanisation" must also be regarded in that more constructive light which sees scientific and technological advances as a humanisation of nature.

It was from this positive and more hopeful position that the Battelle-American Assembly of 1963 [12] discussed problems arising from the impact on society of automation and technological change. It described important technological trends not only as expressions of increasing human ability (the growing mastery of new areas of space and energy) and man's deeper penetration into the nature of matter (increasing ability to extend and control the life of the natural world), but also as an extension of man's sensory capabilities and intelligence. For his vision is extended by radar, by the electron microscope and radio astronomy; his hearing operates at ever greater depths through amplification techniques; his touch is extended by instrumentation and control combinations which identify minute or distant conditions and provide for a human response that will change them. His augmented powers of perception, and the notion of discrimination—of the more careful identification of environment—which inheres in them, are accompanied by the subtle and significant extension of man's memory through increased ability to preserve visual and aural impressions; and extended memory is now matched by the mechanised exploration of complex mathematical relationships in which the computer—extended intelligence—works with fantastic improvement in accuracy and thoroughness over all man's intelligence more immediately applied in this field.

Of course, by stating the depressingly and magnificently obvious, it is possible to deepen the mystery of this physical-

[12] *Automation and Technological Change*, Proceedings published by Battelle Memorial Institute, July, 1963.

nonphysical relationship of man to the world outside: for in order to live he must eat. Yet the same calories seem as indifferent as they are necessary to the spiritual values they nourish. Energies of mind and matter are constantly associated, and in some way pass into each other, but it is impossible to establish the correspondence between them. A little food may enable the highest exercise of intellectual energy! Could it be that a single energy sustains the world?

We have now looked briefly at two aspects of the soul: at the polarity between mind and body, and the tension between man and the world; and find that neither antithesis can be clearly and precisely maintained. The tendency of experience to group itself about the material and the immaterial, exerting attractive and repulsive energies upon each other, allows of no clear distinction between body and soul.

Occasionally philosophy and theology have presented the soul as being uniquely and independently created, and capable of separate existence, but they must concede that this is a *conceptual* statement and may be believed. What we are able to know points to this: the soul is inseparable in its birth and growth from those forms of being which we experience. Those who prefer to differentiate between the "soul" of theology and the sum total of what we actually and potentially experience, that is to say, the "psyche" of psychology, must find themselves hard pressed to give the theological "soul" any meaning lying outside human experience and reflection. And if this "soul" is still to be attributed to "supernatural" causes, we must reflect that the Christian doctrine of creation attributes all events, ultimately, to supernatural causes; and in some instances the doctrine will proceed to declare that supernatural and

49

natural are not mutually exclusive concepts but complementary. If, in this case, the "revelation" of the soul's unique origins is perceived by the human psyche, other grounds may well have to be sought in order to establish the authority of the revelation.

This view of the soul as the organiser of the body and its incorporeal tenant, must lose ground as increasing attention is paid to the "wisdom of the body."

For a layman in these matters, it is impressive to notice how the category of consciousness finds its way into unexpected areas of the life sciences. The zoology section of the 1957 British Association meetings concerned itself with cancer research, and drew attention to the fact that unlike those cells which proliferate round the edge of a wound but cease multiplying when the wound is repaired, cancer cells "run wild" in the body. Whereas healthy cells adhere, surface to surface, in such a manner as to impede further multiplication, the unhealthy are not so inhibited. The central characteristic of biological systems is that they are self-controlling and repairing, which makes it difficult to understand them solely within the concepts of physics and chemistry. Their behaviour depends upon some form of memory. The view was put forward, therefore, that cancer cells may have "forgotten" how to behave in the body, or the body has "forgotten" how to control them.[13]

When we reflect that the struggle for new concepts lies at the heart of scientific advancement, not least in importance is the mnemonic category in the study of control mechanisms (cybernetics) in relation to biological systems!

In his book entitled *The Uniqueness of the Individual,* P. B. Medawar says that "skin homografts are destroyed by

[13] Professor J. Z. Young's presidential address, British Association (Zoology Section).

an immunological reaction" (a process fundamentally akin to that which is provoked by bacterial, viral or cellular infections), yet "embryos will accept homografts because they are not yet old enough to have acquired an immunologial conscience, to have learned the difference between what is native to them and what is foreign." Indeed, "foreign cells introduced into an embryo affect it in such a way that it may never acquire the power to recognise the cells as foreign, and may accept them as its own." [14]

In a symposium entitled "The Nature of Sleep," it has been suggested that "instead of being central in sleep, the brain is the servant of the body in that state." The need for sleep, it was said, arose elsewhere in the body than in the brain, and "what the brain does in succumbing to sleep is teleologically what the brain should do in submitting to a resting process." [15] When the body is paralysed by sleep, the brain is more open to danger from any source than it is in the conscious state when the body is all attuned to the possibility of danger and therefore of immediate action. Contrary to unreflective opinion there are times and seasons in which the body takes care of the mind!

Within the experience of a majority of people a sudden emergency is met by doing the saving thing before their minds have grasped the situation. We jump away from the oncoming traffic, leaving our minds surprised that we have done so. Our hands have caught the fragile cup before our minds are fully aware of its fall, let alone able to issue orders for its rescue. We often attribute these immediate actions to instinct, but their source is described by Jules Fabre as "life's crowning mental gift," and by the Spanish

[14] (London: Methuen, 1957), p. 152.
[15] *Times* (London), medical correspondent, 27th October, 1961.

neurologist Cajal as "mind with instant and decisive action." [16]

This description of body and soul, mind and matter, appears to render "all distinctions void" by asserting that these distinctions, though useful, are not fundamental, but it must be clear that this does not represent a return to the poetic and allegorical unity described in former times, for example by Lucretius in his *De rerum natura*. Reasoned argument and confirmed observation describing the behaviour of the earth and man find them to be one homogeneous system. "All their acts are manifestations of a 'doing' or 'power' which it traces to be fundamentally of one kind throughout." [17]

We may say in drawing the strands of this chapter together that the monistic view of our existence which, as Idealism (extremely expressed as solipsism), seeks to absorb matter into mind or, as Materialism, wishes to dissolve the soul in the body is not a satisfactory understanding of our experience. Solipsism is irresistibly contradicted by the effrontery of having to maintain that the rest of the world and its inhabitants emanate from "me" like a mirage and are otherwise without reality. Materialism seems to forget that matter is never presented to us directly and that we deal only with sensory impressions; that the phenomena described by natural science are psychical experiences and not things in themselves.

Those who hold dualistic views maintain either that body and soul live parallel but independent lives (cf. Occasionalism), or that they are two semi-independent entities, associated in psychosomatic interaction, but capable of

[16] Quoted by Sir Charles Sherrington, *Man on His Nature* (London: Pelican, 1955), p. 117.
[17] *Ibid.*, p. 243.

separate existence. This view shows vigour where it is sustained by concrete conceptions of the soul; elsewhere it becomes impossible to hold. The representation of ourselves as consisting of an immortal soul in a mortal body, the body being material like the earth and the soul immaterial and without earthly counterpart, is not a true symbolism of the life we know. If matter and spirit are really incongruous, there can be no relationship between them; body-mind relationships become unthinkable. Life, however, denies this impasse. And if there is no recognition of "spirit" in a material world, and no place for "matter" in a spiritual world, it emerges that "matter" and "spirit" have been misconceived, and that life requires us to regard them as necessary and complementary aspects of a reality which embraces and transcends both.

"Men are not machines, not even ghost-ridden machines. They are men. . . ." [18] It is not possible to uphold trichotomous man as body, soul and spirit, with its ground in the soul as the permanent reality of the self—a view falsely attributed to the Bible and to the Greeks. Human reality, the self which is neither body nor soul, is a mysterious dialectic of physical and psychical relationships of which the contours of the body are certainly not a true frontier. There is an exterior environment, the world of sensible phenomena which surrounds and supports us, and an interior environment, the world of our ideas, imaginations, desires and feelings. None can define where one ends and the other begins; none can trace the dividing line, and none can say to what degree we are of the exterior world or describe the extent to which that world participates in our inwardness.

[18] Gilbert Ryle, *The Concept of Mind* (London: Hutchinson; London University Library series, 1959), p. 81.

3

Sight and Touch

We don't exist unless we are deeply and sensually in touch with that which can be touched but not known.

D. H. Lawrence [1]

> *Are not these woods*
> *More free from peril than the envious court?*
> *Here feel we but the penalty of Adam,*
> *The season's difference; as the icy fang*
> *And churlish chiding of the winter's wind,*
> *Which, when it bites and blows upon my body,*
> *Even till I shrink with cold, I smile and say*
> *"This is no flattery: these are counsellors*
> *That feelingly persuade me what I am."*
>
> *William Shakespeare* [2]

> *You will not see the world at first:*
> *you will touch flesh and you will cry.*
> *Years later you will cry because*
> *you see too much and touch too little.*
>
> *Edwin Brock* [3]

MARTIN BUBER'S "life of monologue" is not one of apparent solitude, but human life enclosed upon itself, in which a man fails to recognise that he is being addressed, through varieties of forms and in many ways, by the contiguous reality in which he has his being. The man who leads a

[1] "Non-Existence" in *Complete Poems*, III (London: Heinemann, 1939), p. 41.

[2] *As You Like It*, Act II, scene 1.

[3] "D-day Minus," *The Listener* (London), 28th November, 1963.

monologic life regards his natural surroundings either as a state of soul or as a passive object of knowledge; either he brings nature idealistically within his own soul, or he isolates it realistically from himself. His surroundings never become for him "a word apprehended with senses of beholding and feeling." [4]

In contrast to this life turned in upon itself is the "life of dialogue," whose basic movement is a turning towards "the other." This turning, however, not only represents a man's intention of establishing a living mutual relationship between himself and the particular person with whom he has to do, but also contains an attitude of openness to nature, an ability to "experience the other side." And this companionship of creation is an essential element in the life of dialogue; it belongs to authentic human existence.

The following autobiographical writing, which relates to Buber's childhood, illustrates this companionship clearly. He describes how the eleven-year-old boy, spending summer in the country, would steal unobserved into the stable in order to stroke the neck of a broad dapple-grey horse, and how this was not a casual delight, but a deeply stirring event within the friendship which existed between them.

If I am to explain it now, beginning from the still very fresh memory of my hand, I must say that what I experienced in touch with the animal was the Other, the immense otherness of the Other, which, however, did not remain strange like the otherness of the ox and the ram, but rather let me draw near and touch it. When I stroked the mighty mane . . . and felt the life beneath my hand, it was as though the element of vitality itself bordered on my skin, something that was not I, was certainly not akin to me, palpably the other, not just another,

⁴ Buber *Between Man and Man* (London: Routledge & Kegan Paul, 1947), p. 20.

really the Other itself; and yet it let me approach, confided itself to me, placed itself elementally in the relation of *Thou* and *Thou* with me.[5]

But this remarkable degree of communication did not last. The child became conscious of the action of stroking the horse, and because he withdrew into himself and became to some extent an observer of their meeting, the experience lost its directness; its actuality gave place to a state in which he reflected upon it. In the first phase of the relationship, however, a tangible object (the mighty mane), through the medium of touch (the element of vitality bordered on my skin), participates in bringing about an awareness of "the Other"; it constitutes an essential element in "experiencing the other side," and plays a vital role in the meeting within which man is addressed. It becomes a sign of man's relatedness to the reality in which he exists.

With this quality of awareness in mind we shall now consider something of the significance of the external world as it stimulates bodily sensations: the sensation of sight, and particularly the sensation of touch.

Albrecht Dürer described sight as "the noblest sense of man," and vision undoubtedly yields the most precise and detailed perception of the world about us. But it does not quite succeed in coming to grips with things. The importance of the sense of touch was vaguely hinted at in ancient times. In *The Sophist* the discussion concerns being and nonbeing; and Plato likens one party to the argument to those Giants who, at war with the Olympians, literally clutch at rocks and trees in order to drag all things down from heaven to earth: "With their grasp tight on such objects they persist in asseverating that nothing *is* but what

[5] *Ibid.*, pp. 52–53.

resists the touch and can be handled." [6]

Western philosophy has rarely pursued this suggestion, but Condillac, whom we associate with the French Enlightenment, in his *Treatise on the Sensations,* maintained that though the combination of smell, hearing, taste and sight multiplies the range of our attention, our pleasure and desires, it does not produce a judgement of externality, and must leave us without a suspicion either that we have bodies or that they are modified by outside causes.[7] In other words, originally the sense of touch is responsible for our judgements of the physical and material world.[8] Condillac points out that the habit of judging distance, motion, size and shape by sight has inclined us to think that these judgements are due to sight alone, but that this is not the case: the eye learns these arts in conjunction with the sense of touch.[9] It is when touch is associated with the other senses that man discovers his own sense organs and judges that sensations relate to external objects.

More recent exploration into the nature and significance of our tactile sense has yielded interesting results. Within the disciplines of anthropology and human biology, M. F. Ashley Montagu read a paper entitled "Non-Verbal Communication: The Mind of the Skin." [10] In this he questioned the purposes for which certain mammals lick the skin

[6] *The Sophist and The Statesman,* trans. with an introduction by A. E. Taylor (Edinburgh: T. Nelson and Sons, 1961), p. 143 (246A).

[7] Etienne Bonnot de Condillac, *Traité des Sensations,* trans. G. Carr (Los Angeles: University of Southern California, 1930), I. xii. 2; cf. Part II: "Touch, the only sense which of itself can judge of externality."

[8] *Ibid.,* II. v. 4 and 5.

[9] *Ibid.,* III. iv. 2.

[10] University of California (Berkeley), 17th October, 1963. Cf. also Margaret A. Ribble, *The Rights of Infants* (New York: Columbia University Press, 1943) pp. 35–42.

of their young immediately upon birth, and found that this was not a cleansing device but the initial movement in a communication process through the skin and its nerve beginnings. Human beings and their colateral relatives, the primates, do not lick their young, who nevertheless undergo an equivalent cutaneous stimulation during the lengthier period of labour through which they pass in being born. This communication through the skin relates to the functioning of the urogenital and gastro-intestinal tracts. Unlicked animals do not survive because these physiological systems, which should have been alerted by stimulation, are never roused to action. Caesarian-born children, the manner of whose birth circumvents the sensory experience encountered during labour, have been shown to suffer later from bowel and bladder deficiencies. Human babies are rather like marsupials, who arrive before gestation is complete, but they have no pouch within which the process may be accomplished. The mothers of so-called primitive peoples, who carry and suckle their offspring much further into childhood than do their more "civilised" relatives, bestow a birthright upon their young with a liberality denied to children in more "advanced" cultures. The absence of this prolonged stimulation of the skin carries verifiable consequences for body and mind. The tactual fondling of an infant, therefore, is more than the mere stroking of the skin; it is the stimulation of sources of energy and a communication of life.

Recent considerations of the sense of touch in the context of perception as a whole have led to the disclosure of interesting data, and some of these deductions represent important points upon the frontier we are now exploring.

Consider the difference between the sense of touch and the other four senses. In the case of sight, sound, taste and smell, we possess sense organs directly associated with these forms of perceiving. In the case of our tactual sense, we have no particular organ to which it is related, but find that the surface of the entire body and also the tongue acts as our "organ" of touch.

The second difference is that touch involves feeling. The eye is not aware of itself in seeing, nor the ear in hearing, nor the nose in smelling, nor the tongue in tasting, but what we perceive by touch is a direct contact with the sensitive surface of the body. The "organ" of perception is itself immediately perceived; we become aware of our own bodily state.

In judging the size and position of things in our environment we *see* them related to our bodies, but we do not compare their shape or colour, for example, in this way. In the case of touch everything is related to our bodies. Heaviness and lightness relate to strength; hardness and softness to the condition of our flesh and bones; always, in touch, we are aware of a relation between our bodies and whatever impinges upon them.

Although touch is less frequently illusory, it is also less accurate than sight. The discovery of shape, for example, yields more readily to sight than to touch. Yet sight reveals a world of "visual" objects while touch relates us directly to our physical environment; it gives immediate perception in contrast to that mediate awareness of things which sight affords. In this respect sound, taste [11] and smell

[11] The tongue shares with the skin a tactile sense, but possesses taste buds and papillae for tasting.

resemble sight rather than touch; their organs are not themselves involved in the immediate perception of material things, but with data which correspond with things.

The physical contact involved in touch but absent from vision requires us to define the comparison more clearly, and we notice that the sense of touch relates both to pressure and to the idea of one thing making another thing happen. Sight, of course, may always be an onlooker; it may see one thing coming into contact with another, and may observe the physical displacements which follow. But touch alone experiences the actual pressures contained in displacement. Touch alone is immediately aware of the causal transaction that occurs.

When, therefore, we seek to know how we become aware of the world that exists outside ourselves, we are confronted first with tactual evidence. In this respect touch is prior to vision, for it operates in direct contact with the world, while sight operates only at a distance and through the medium of light. Touch relates immediately to things, while sight engages with sense data; and if we ask how we become aware of existents other than ourselves, and answer, By thinking about them!—then the world about us is simply whatever we think about when we think, and no bridge spans the gulf between thought and existence, for thought is encapsuled within its own thought world.[12]

The fundamental nature of the sense of touch becomes

[12] The following works deal with the subject of touch at greater length: D. M. Armstrong, *Bodily Sensations* (London: Routledge & Kegan Paul, 1962); John Macmurray's Gifford Lectures, 1953–54: *The Self as Agent*, pp. 104–26 and *Persons in Relation*, pp. 44–85 (London: Faber and Faber, 1957 and 1961) Macmurray reiterates Condillac's view that "the primary perception of the Other . . . is tactual"; Maine de Biran, *The Influence of Habit on the Faculty of Thinking* (Baltimore: Williams and Wilkins, 1929).

more pronounced when we recognize that loss of sight does not rob us of the capacity for knowing the world about us. Even the man born blind may grow up to know the world and to direct his life in accordance with his disability. It is no doubt possible to imagine a human being without tactual sense, but such a person could not exist. He would "infallibly perish." [13] Physiological considerations make his survival unthinkable. But were his existence even possible, how could such a man know that he was surrounded by a world of things, or that his body itself was composed of actual flesh and blood? He would be quite enclosed within a world of the imagination, of ideas, without power to differentiate between the pictures in his mind and the perception of a material world.

Experience has taught us, sometimes bitterly, that the core of tactual perception is resistance. The feeling of pressure which occurs within our bodies, particularly at the point or area of contact, is a sense datum, but the resistance itself is a factual thing. It is the immediate apprehension of the external world. Sometimes we offer resistance to things, and at other times they offer resistance to us. We swim against the tide and offer resistance to its power over our bodies. The door refuses to open and resists our intention of passing through it. The harder we press, the stiffer the resistance. Yet it is in this experience of resistance between our bodies and the apparently recalcitrant objects of our environment that we are enabled to identify ourselves as existing "in the flesh." In the experience of what is not ourselves we discover simultaneously our own physical selves.

It would be petulant, then, to interpret the resistance occasioned by contact with our physical environment

[13] Condillac, *Traité des Sensations,* II. viii. 1.

merely as frustration or a hindrance to personal designs because the external world makes physical self-awareness possible, while its actual pressures upon us, both resisting and supporting our movements, constitute the experience itself. The sense of touch requires contingent environment, and is meaningless without its complementary physical milieu.

That tactual perception is primary for our self-understanding is more clearly recognised in the case of newly born children responding to their earliest surroundings. Human babies appear in the world quite helplessly dependent upon those who will nurture them; their survival depends upon human care, and without it they must die. Their sole adaptation to environment is to be unadapted to it, apart from the ability to communicate feelings of discomfort by crying. The child cries, and the motivation of its crying contains an implicit reference to its mother, and when this impulse to communicate draws the mother's appropriate attention, the mother-child relationship thus established is an original unit of personal existence.

With this "you and I" relationship the process of learning to perceive the world of objects begins. The child's first perception of its mother is tactual; he learns the comfort of the mother's physical presence in the actions of her caring. Repeated crying calls forth repeated tactual contact, and this behaviour pattern elicits recognition from the child. The pale light of memory and expectation herald the dawn of consciousness. And in the child's growing awareness of the difference between tactual care and the absence of it lie the first traces of discrimination and knowledge of a material world.

In the life of every human being, therefore, knowledge of the personal precedes knowledge of that which is not-personal, for the world of our first childhood is responsive. In those now distant surroundings we began to differentiate between what answered our cries and what did not; and from the immediate, tactually responsive world of "you and I" we began to abstract the occasions which bore no response to our calling; from repeated discrimination an "it and I" relationship emerged, and gradually a world of objects was born.

But this process of learning was first tactual, and before our eyes acquired skill in focussing attention, and random movements gave way to the location and handling of objects in space, sight learned to correlate itself with touch. Now that we have become used to apprehending "things" it is hard to conceive of a condition in which the distinction between animate and inanimate objects was not obvious. When we are confronted with a personal apprehension of the material world, as in poetry or in primitive nature-worship, we explain it as a personification of what we "normally" regard as inanimate. In the story of our lives, however, the reverse of this is true: we arrived at the concept of an inanimate world by abstracting it from a responsive world; the material world emerged as an unresponsive or depersonalised part of that originally wholly responsive world of the mother-child relationship. This personal apprehension of environment which we tend to regard as superficially emotional or as a matter of sentiment rather than material interest must begin to acquire credibility and value once we recognise the genetic priority of a tactually apprehended responsive world.

Students of ecology speak of a unity which binds all nature's manifestations together with an intimacy that is both vitally necessary and frequently mutual. And without denying man's freedom to act we may rightly observe that his natural environment has played a significant part in prescribing the nature of his activities and the forms of his culture.

It is said that whereas the landscape of Italy smiles, soft and caressing, that of Greece stares, challenging and tough. It is a land reduced to its essentials, where few trees offer shade and the light gives no halftones but penetrates everything, pervades everything, and mercilessly reveals the most hidden crannies. In a land dominated by the sun's strength, and in which environment forces itself with strength and clarity upon man's awareness, it is perhaps to be expected that the Greeks established the primacy of sight within the family of our senses. In doing so they made the optical world *the* world to which the data provided by the other senses might usefully contribute, and their thinking bears an optical character. Martin Buber describes the history of Greek philosophy as "an opticizing of thought" [14] but we must hasten to add that this concentration of attention upon vision is neither mere habit nor an arbitrary choice on the part of philosophers, but has its roots in the actual importance of sight in daily life. Thus vision has tended to be the model upon which all knowledge is construed. Thought itself is an inner vision, and self-transcendence a looking upon oneself. Contemplation is reflection, and the basis of science is observation. When we reflect upon the world disclosed to our senses, it is usual to think of the world we see with our eyes. Our vision casts objects upon the screen of the world before us; we become observers and stand over against the viewed world as subjects before an object. And distance intervenes across which our seeing does not affect

[14] *The Eclipse of God* (London: Gollancz, 1953), p. 56.

the object, for seeing is receptivity: it is a withdrawal from the direct contact contained in action.

Our relatedness to the world in terms of vision produces a kind of knowledge which can be described as interpretation; the extent and greatness of this knowledge is now beyond the power of any one person to conceive. But despite the fruitfulness of this relationship, failure both to recognise the significance of tactual sense and to participate more immediately in the actuality of the world by doing leaves us unnecessarily impoverished. For between the knowing that is reflection and the actual world there must always be distance; the knowing that springs from action and enfolds reflection within itself brings subject and object together across the intervening space, for in the realm of doing our mental and physical worlds are one.

C. F. von Weizsäcker, writing about the procedures of atomic physics,[15] states that the atom itself is not immediately perceived. It is not given as an object in space and time, for it is not possible fully to describe its nature in spatio-temporal terms. The atom behaves in some experiments like a spatially concentrated particle (Newton), and in others like a wave filling the whole of space (Huyghens), but it cannot at one and the same time be both wave and particle. This logical paradox is avoided by the fact that it is impossible to conduct experiments upon an atom so that it reacts simultaneously in these two ways. If the atom discloses its wave properties, then its particle properties may be predicted only with probability; if its particle properties are known, then its other magnitudes such as wave length, are only predictable with probability. It is not possible to

[15] *The World View of Physics* (London: Routledge & Kegan Paul, 1952), pp. 32 ff.

say that the atom is a particle or that it is a wave but simply that it is either a particle or a wave, and that the way in which it manifests itself rests upon the disposition of the experiment.

When we look at things in one way, we destroy simultaneously the alternative ways of seeing them, so that this apparent incompatibility does not reflect the capriciousness of the atom, nor does it mean that the reality of things depends upon man's arbitrary choice, but that the picture in terms of which we understand reality depends upon the way in which the physicist presses the atom to disclose itself. Also, the two mutually incompatible definitions of the atom as a spatially continuous-discontinuous event show that nature is not completely objectifiable, that it is not simply extended in space, and that the category of "substance" must yield to an understanding of nature as bearing an event-character.

The event must be observed in order to be known, but the act of observation changes the nature of the event. In terms of vision, however, "the act of observation" does not appear to be capable of changing anything; but when observation means "getting in touch with," the possibility of change emerges. And von Weizsäcker says elsewhere in his book: "Every experiment is an act of violence which we impose on nature. It must react to the violence." [16]

The view that in observation and perception subject and object are inextricably interwoven has often been dominated by the idea that direct physical impressions are caused by the object in the subject or observer. We must now understand that unavoidable and uncontrollable impressions occur from the side of the subject upon the object. We cannot obtain knowledge of objects without making

[16] *Ibid.*, p. 57.

contact with them; but in so doing we disturb them, and they disturb us. Our relationship with our environment is one of interaction, or transaction.[17]

The surrounding world does not contain its own explanation. When we seek to understand it, the character of *the* knowledge it yields up reflects our own thinking and the path by which we ourselves travelled to the point of disclosure. We do not see things as *they* are, but as *we* are.

Archimedes was convinced that given standing room outside he would be able to move the world. No such place is required for this task. Our contact with the world allows us to glimpse the most mysterious and terrifying feature of our cognitive powers: our capacities for knowing possess the power to change the world.

It is important to see that all sense perception is not passive receptivity to impressions. Vision may tend to give us a picture of reality which is divided between subject and object, but the tactual enquiries of atomic physics make us aware of our intimate, interacting relationship with the world which, when it discloses itself, enfolds simultaneously the mind and the will and the faith of men who can know only as they act and create.

The sense of touch, then, employed either directly or in its extended form through scientific experiment, expresses a creative relationship with the world. This creative power, together with his freedom, is the cradle of man's fears for his future; how he touches the world and with what spiritual qualities he handles matter will be of lasting significance.

We shall look more closely at the proposition that our indissoluble union with things means that they acquire a spiritual meaning; for the moment it is interesting to recall

[17] John Dewey, *Logic: The Theory of Inquiry* (New York: Henry Holt, 1938), Chap. XXV.

a passage in John Steinbeck's *The Grapes of Wrath* in which he compares a qualitative difference in man's attitude to the soil and its consequences in both men and things. He describes first the impersonal cultivation of the land by a monster tractor, operated by a driver "gloved, goggled, rubber dust-mask over nose and mouth" who could not see the land as it was or smell its earthiness, whose feet did not stamp the clods or feel the warmth and power of the ground, but from an iron seat methodically raped the land without passion.

And when the crop grew, and was harvested, no man had crumbled a hot clod in his fingers and let the earth sift past his finger-tips. No man had touched the seed or lusted for the growth. Men ate what they had not raised, had no connection with the bread. The land bore under iron, and under iron gradually died; for it was not loved or hated, it had no prayers or curses.[18]

But the local tenant, whose land had been so affronted ponders the strange "companionship of creation":

If a man owns a little property, that property is him, it's part of him, and it's like him. If he owns property only so he can walk on it and handle it and be sad when it isn't doing well, and feel fine when the rain falls on it, that property is him, and in some way he's bigger because he owns it. Even if he isn't successful he's big with his property. That is so.[19]

And Steinbeck carefully notes the factual but unfortunate truth of a less personal relationship to the soil, in which a man is diminished by the property he neither sees, walks upon, nor handles with his fingers, whose relationship with the earth is reduced from companionship to servitude.

[18] (New York: Viking Press, 1939), p. 48.
[19] *Ibid.*, pp. 50–51.

4

The Truth of Things

Only few consider the truth which resides in the essence of things.

Anselm [1]

I call an amateur *in philosophy anyone who accepts the terms of a usual problem as they are. . . . . doing philosophy authentically would consist in creating the framework of the problem and of creating the solution.*

Henri Bergson [2]

LUCIEN LÉVY-BRUHL tells us that an essential trait of primitive mentality is its strangeness to abstract thought. It refrains from reasoning, and in this it is prelogical though not antilogical. The primitive makes no distinction between what is actually present to his senses and what is beyond them. "At the very moment when he perceives what is presented to his senses, the primitive represents to himself the mystic force which is manifesting itself thus." [3]

This primitive awareness of the world, which Lévy-Bruhl has called "participation mystique," appears not to arise from desire for a rational explanation of the universe, but originates, rather, as a response to collective needs and

[1] "De Veritate," Chap. IX, in *Anselmi Opera Omnia* (Edinburgh: T. Nelson and Sons, 1946), I, p. 188: *"Veritatem vero quae est in rerum essentia, pauci considerant."*

[2] Quoted by M. Merleau-Ponty, *In Praise of Philosophy* (Evanston, Ill., Northwestern University Press, 1963), p. 14.

[3] *Primitive Mentality* (London: Allen and Unwin, 1923), p. 60.

sentiments. On this ground it is wrong to suggest that primitive people simply associate magical properties or occult powers with all the objects that affect their senses or strike their imagination, and that in a word, they are animists. He insists that it is not a question of the association of the physical with the nonphysical, that it is not a matter of animism but of dynamism. The real but imperceptible forces with which all things and all beings are imbued are integral to the whole. It is only at a later stage of social evolution that natural phenomena tend to become the sole content of sense perception to the exclusion of the mystic qualities which then assume the character of beliefs and, finally, of superstitions. Participation mystique represents an awareness of life prior to this dissociation in which the perception of sense data and what is beyond them remain an undifferentiated whole.[4]

In the primitive mind, therefore, nature and man do not stand in opposition to one another ("the piece of land on which a group of human beings lives is the group itself"[5]), and do not have to be apprehended by different modes of cognition.

Contrary to participation mystique—life built up within a narrow circle of acts highly charged with presentness—there is in the thought of civilised man a basic distinction between what is regarded as subjective and that which is termed objective. On this distinction scientific thought has based its critical and analytical procedures by which it is able progressively to reduce individual phenomena to typical events subject to universal laws. In this way it can

[4] Cf. L. Lévy-Bruhl, *How Natives Think* (London: Allen and Unwin, 1926), pp. 44–45.
[5] Lévy-Bruhl, *Primitive Mentality*, p. 446.

hardly avoid creating an increasingly wide gulf between our perception of the phenomenal world and the conceptions by which we make it understandable. Sunrise and sunset bring to mind earth's rotation. Colours are wavelengths. And we accept these descriptions because they can be shown to possess a greater degree of objectivity than our sense perceptions. But unlike us, primitive man could not withdraw from the presence of the phenomena to which he was related with curious directness, so that the distinction between subjective and objective knowledge was meaningless to him.[6]

Lucien Lévy-Bruhl makes an interesting assessment of these two kinds of awareness of reality.[7] Logical thought permits of no contradiction, yet the phenomenon of prelogical thought, which is indifferent to the claims of reason, surviving largely undisturbed alongside a logical system of concepts, seems to indicate to him that the satisfactions derived from a logical mode of apprehension are incomplete. Compared with conscious ignorance, of course, logical apprehension undoubtedly means a kind of possession of its object, but in comparison with the degree of participation realized by prelogical mentality, logical apprehension gives but part-possession, for knowing in general means to objectify, to project beyond oneself so that knower and object stand in an external relationship to one another.

How intimate is the communion between entities participating in each other, which collective representations of prelogical mentality ensure. It is of the essence of participation that all idea of duality is effaced; in spite of the contra-

[6] Cf. Henri Frankfort, *Before Philosophy* (London: Pelican Books, 1949), p. 20.
[7] *How Natives Think*, pp. 383 f.

dictoriness upon which the logical mind would fasten, the subject is at the same time himself and the being in whom he participates. Comparing the warm assurance of intrinsic possession with the cold certainty of objectifying apprehension, Lévy-Bruhl suggests that this may be the source of those anti-intellectual doctrines which make a periodic, historical appearance promising intimate contact with being, and a communion of subject with object which formal reasoning can never achieve. Even among more highly civilised peoples the need for participation is perhaps more imperious and profound than our thirst for knowledge conformable with reason; we seem to aspire to a knowledge deeper than that which reflection alone can bring, to a participation in being which shall not obliterate but encompass and perfect us.

Apart from the emergence of self-awareness in childhood it is impossible to say precisely how this apprehension of man and the whole as a felt unity was first broken down into subjective and objective aspects of reality, at what point self-awareness became an awareness of self over against the world, or under what pressure the self withdrew from participation into contemplation, yet this is how civilised man for the most part experiences the world.[8]

That our childhood recognition of the distinction between persons and things comes considerably later than our differentiation between persons, and that primitive man's participation mystique precedes the dualism of the world of subject and object, argues that the concept of a material world is derivative, that it is an abstraction from the world

[8] Cf. descriptions of the process of awakening in M. Buber's *I and Thou* (Edinburgh: T. & T. Clark, 1937), Part I; and E. Fromm's *Escape from Freedom* (New York: Farrar and Rinehart, 1941), Chap. II.

in which men act and have their being, and that it is a viewpoint maintained in a position of withdrawal from the world. For what is known in reflection is a mental construction; to *exist* is to be in dynamic interrelation with other existents. If we say, then, that the material world is a nonpersonal world, our knowledge of the material presupposes knowledge of the personal, and the I-Thou relationship of primitive man in a personal world has been superseded by the I-It relationship of civilised man in a material world. It is also apposite to recall what Martin Buber said of these relationships, that "the I of the primary word I-Thou is a different I from that of the primary word I-It." [9]

The participation mystique of our primitive ancestors is now either so deeply submerged in the Unconscious of civilised men, or so withdrawn into self-awareness over against an external world, as to be beyond investigation except where anthropological studies of remaining primitive men are still possible. We may look perhaps more discerningly at some of the ecological relationships of their civilised successors and note not only the estrangement which the earth has endured, but also the renewal of an awareness of man's essential relations with things.

The earliest thinkers of Greek antiquity were predominantly cosmologists and, according to Nietzsche, were still concerned with the "mystic intuition" that "everything is one," assuming a harmony between the external and the internal worlds. They began to reflect upon their observations of the world, speculated about its nature, and occasionally made deductions which anticipated scientific hypotheses of modern times; but they represent a prescientific phase of thought. Their interest in nature was superseded in

[9] *I and Thou,* p. 3.

the minds of those who followed them by an interest in man. The Sophists, Socrates and Plato represent this shift of emphasis from nature to man.

Plato did not omit to give some account of the material universe, and described it as a cosmos ordered by intelligence. Existing disordered material was arranged by the divine Craftsman or Demiurge in accordance with an ideal and eternal pattern, and fashioned by him into a "living creature with soul and reason." [10] Some matter, however, remained intractable and imperfectly subordinated to the operations of reason. Plato could say that "truth is the noblest quality in existing things," but that the soul is the "oldest and most divine of all things." [11]

The understanding—predominant, though not universally held among the Greeks—of the inferiority of matter in relation to spirit has haunted the European mind throughout the centuries. With respect to Christianity we may say that from the moment it was said that "the Word became flesh," matter and spirit were understood to be one whole; henceforth, matter was not to be regarded as a drag upon the human spirit but, rather, as indispensable to it. Exception has been taken to the term "incarnation" on the ground that it reflected Greek rather than Hebrew thinking, but early Christianity required no encouragement to re-divide reality, for it was soon attacked by an "ascetic virus" which perverted the spirit of its Scriptures and invaded the Church from Gnostic and Manichaean sources, which saw in matter, in human flesh and blood, nothing more or less than the substance of a festering evil.

[10] Reflected by Aristotle in *De anima*, III. 8. 431b: the soul "in some way is all things."

[11] *Republic*, VII. 532c, in *The Dialogues of Plato*, III, p. 235.

Section 5 of the explanations and remarks appended to Feuerbach's *Essence of Christianity* begins in this way: "Nature, the world, has no value, no interest for Christians. The Christian thinks only of himself, and the salvation of his soul." [12] This accusation of self-centredness was not entirely fair, nor was it a reasonable deduction to be drawn from the indifference of Christians to nature. That Christians disregarded the natural world was, however, a just contention which Feuerbach had no difficulty in documenting from patristic sources.[13]

[12] Trans. from second German edition by Marian Evans (New York: C. Blanchard, 1855), p. 361.

[13] Arnobius, *Against the Heathen*, Book II, 61 (*Ante-Nicene Fathers*, VI), p. 457: "Whether the sun is larger than the earth, or measures only a foot in breadth: whether the moon shines with borrowed light, or from her own brightness,—things which there is neither profit in knowing, nor loss in not knowing. . . . Your person is not permitted to involve you in such questions, and to be busied to no purpose about things so much out of reach. Your interests are in jeopardy,—the salvation, I mean, of your souls."

Lactantius, *The Divine Institutes*, Book III, viii (*Ante-Nicene Fathers*, VII), p. 76: "I ask, therefore, to what subject knowledge is to be referred. If to the causes of natural things, what happiness will be proposed to me, if I shall know the sources of the Nile, or the vain dreams of the natural philosophers respecting the heaven? Why should I mention that on these subjects there is no knowledge, but mere conjecture, which varies according to the abilities of men?"

Augustine, *Of the Morals of the Catholic Church*, Chap. xxi (*Nicene and Post-Nicene Fathers*, IV), p. 52: "For some people, neglecting virtues, and ignorant of what God is, and of the majesty of the nature which remains always the same, think that they are engaged in an important business when searching with the greatest inquisitiveness and eagerness into this material mass which we call the world. . . . The soul, then, which purposes to keep itself chaste for God must refrain from the desire of vain knowledge like this. For this desire usually produces delusion, so that the soul thinks that nothing exists but what is material; or if, from regard to authority it confesses that there is an immaterial existence, it can think of it only under material images, and has no belief regarding it but that imposed by the bodily sense."

Ambrose, *Hexameron*, I, vi (New York: The Fathers of the Church, 1961): "On the nature and position of the earth there should be no need

75

Over against this disparagement of nature we hear voices raised from time to time, attempting to reaffirm the Christian estimate of the dignity of matter. Anselm of Canterbury, in his *Dialogue concerning Truth,* says, "There is then truth in the essence of all things which are, for they are what they are in the highest truth," [14] yet "only few consider the truth which lies in the essence of things." [15] Thomas Aquinas quotes Augustine to the effect that "the true is that which is," and his own reply to the question, Is there any false thing? states that "all things are true, and nothing is false." [16] To minds steeped in the thought of the neutrality if not the passivity of their physical environment, this Thomistic viewpoint may sound deliberately provocative, and an attempt at its explanation will be made later in the chapter.

For a brief historical moment, Aquinas sought to restore dignity to creation; not to produce factual proof of the truth of existing things (which would hardly be possible), but to draw attention to the power to disclose reality which was inherent in his understanding of the relationship between the mind and the essence of things. Those who followed

---

to enter into discussion at this point with respect to what is to come. It is sufficient for our information to state what the text of the Holy Scriptures establishes, namely, that, 'he hangeth the earth upon nothing.'"

Luther, *Sämmtliche Schriften und Werke,* XIII (Leipzig, 1729), p. 264: "Let natural science alone. . . . It is enough thou knowest fire is hot, water cold and moist. . . . Know how thou oughtest to treat thy field, thy cow, thy house and child—that is enough of natural science for thee. Think how thou mayest learn Christ, who will show thee thyself, who thou art, and what is thy capability. Thus thou wilt learn God and thyself, which no natural master or natural science ever taught."

[14] *De veritate essentiae rerum,* Chap. VII., p. 185: *"Est igitur veritas in omnium quae sunt essentia, quia hoc sunt quod in summa veritate sunt."*

[15] *Ibid.,* Chap. IX.

[16] *Truth (Quaestiones disputatae de veritate),* trans. R. W. Mulligan, S.J. (Chicago: Henry Regnery, 1952), Vol. I, Question 1, Article 10.

him, however, do not appear to have found the "truth of things" a meaningful concept.

In his work entitled *De dignitate et augmentis scientarium,* Francis Bacon has nothing directly to say about the truth of things. And in the transition from Scholasticism to modern philosophy Thomas Hobbes is aware of the Thomistic notion of the nature of things, but considers it trifling and puerile:

Now these words *true, truth* and *true proposition* are equivalent to one another; for truth consists in speech, and not in things spoken of; and . . . *true* . . . is always to be referred to the truth of the proposition. Truth or verity is not any affection of the thing, but of the proposition concerning it.[17]

Descartes envisaged man as composed of thinking substance and corporeal substance but, to preserve the integrity of free mental activity, accorded to mind an origin quite dissociated from matter. The nature of mind is such that it could not have been "educed from matter," and must have been "expressly created." He regarded the body simply as a medium of certain sensations; mutual interaction between mind and body he set in the lowest possible terms.

From that I knew that I was a substance the whole essence or nature of which is to think, and that for its existence there is no need of any place, nor does it depend on any material thing; so that this 'me', that is to say, the soul by which I am what I am, is entirely distinct from body, and is even more easy to know than is the latter; and even if body were not, the soul would not cease to be what it is.[18]

[17] *The English Works of Thomas Hobbes,* ed. Sir William Molesworth (London: J. Bohn, 1839), Vol. I, Chap. 3, Section 7, p. 35.

[18] *Philosophical Works of Descartes,* trans. E. S. Haldane and G. R. T. Ross (New York: Dover, 1931, corrected reprint), Vol. I: *Discourse on Method,* p. 101.

In his fourth Meditation, "Of the True and the False," Descartes confesses that when representations of a corporeal nature present themselves to his mind he wonders whether "this thinking nature which is in me, or rather by which I am what I am, differs from this corporeal nature, or whether both are not simply the same thing." Yet he is able to dismiss the thought with sublime indifference.

Spinoza regards mind and extension as modes of God, but raises the topic of the truth of things only in order to demonstrate that it is nonsensical. Those who have judged truth to be an attribute of existing things have gone completely astray. Truth is only in statement; things are dumb. In his *Principles of Cartesian Philosophy,* the section entitled *"Cogitata metaphysica:* One, the True, the Good," Spinoza asks, "What are the properties of Truth? Certainty is not in things. Those who seek certainty in things themselves are deceived in the same way as when they seek Truth in them. Nor is there need to dwell any longer on these questions." [19]

The Empiricists had managed to dissolve the reality of the world into a host of unrelated feelings or sensations which together, they said, compose the human mind. Yet their scepticism was of a limited and theoretical character, for they would have been fools to eat food made of sense data only, to breathe insubstantial air with unreal lungs, or to walk with unreal feet upon a nonexistent earth towards imaginary goals. So when Hume reduced knowledge to the sense content within the mind, Kant felt it necessary to presuppose a certain framework of thought relationships in order to make real knowledge possible. The sensations we

[19] Trans. H. E. Wedeck (New York: Philosophical Library, 1961), p. 142.

experience are not isolated from one another; they enter a unified consciousness because they pass through a synthesising process in order to become knowledge. The known world, insofar as it is known, is a construct of thought. Objects are built up within these intellectual relationships, so that our experience is no mere string of subjective feelings. The known world is not a datum given by some external power; it is not an objective fact independent of us, but the product of the ways of our understanding.

The relation of thought to its object had frequently been understood in terms of the relation of a copy to its prototype, but Kant made the actual relationship between the external world and the thought world constitutive of knowledge. Between thought and its object, between the world and ourselves, there is no separateness, but an inner identity.

In the second edition of the *Critique of Pure Reason,* supplementary to the table of categories (or pure concepts of understanding) Kant briefly discusses the Scholastic proposition about the unity, truth and perfection of everything (*Quodlibet ens est unum, verum, bonum*), but suggests that the principle yields nothing but tautological propositions. What are supposed to be predicates of things are nothing but logical requirements and criteria of all knowledge of things in general. The Schoolmen used these predicates of unity, truth and perfection in a formal way only, "yet incautiously made these criteria of thought to be properties of things by themselves." [20] But they are simply terms which make possible the definition of objects; they can be subsumed under categories of understanding as elaborations of those mental relations which permit us to

[20] Trans. Max Müller (London: Macmillan, 1915), pp. 739–40.

79

think of objects. For the external world yields only formless stuff which Kant calls "matter." But subjected to "forms of intuition" matter acquires the characteristics which make it recognisable as "things in time and space." Things are further defined by the "principles of understanding" and acquire among other characteristics those of quantity, quality, substance and causality, and become for us "the world of phenomena." Productive imagination, in accordance with the rules of understanding, produces this phenomenal world whose form or order is also the form of our knowing.

From this, we may say that the person experiencing the phenomenal world is the thinker rather than the total man, and that the relationship expressed can be described in Buber's language as the "primary word I-It which can never be spoken with the whole being." The sensations I experience are referred to the object as my representations of it, so that the form of my thought is the form of the object, and truth is objectivity. I perceive the world, and distinguish between it and myself, and this dichotomy of subject-object is the abstract form of my knowledge.

Kant's criticism of the Schoolmen for their incaution in making certain "criteria of thought to be properties of things by themselves" is unjust to Aquinas, whose discussion of things does not trespass beyond the bounds of their relationship either to man's perceiving mind or to the mind of God. Aquinas' "truth of things," like Buber's "primary words," betoken relations; Aquinas is not referring to the existence of things, to their sheer distribution in space, but to their essence, to the whatness of things, to those qualities and patterns of behaviour which the mind reaches out to grasp, to enfold within itself, with which it seeks accord, and believes then to be true.

Thomas' view of the world is contained in *Summa contra Gentiles* (Book IV, chap. xi), and his exposition of the truth of things appears in the *De veritate*. Our natural knowledge of things begins with sensory perception. A human being is not a soul in a body, but an existential unity of body and soul, so that it is not a spiritual part of man which is the ultimate bearer of knowledge, but the total man who is body and soul.

In speaking about this knowing person, Thomas notes the difference between intellect and the senses: while the latter apprehend sense data (phantasms), the intellect "penetrates within." "Now the inwardly conceived word is a kind of form or image of the thing understood"; *our mental images are reflections of the external world;* so that every understood thing, as understood, must be in the one who perceives and understands, for the mind reaches out to those objects it wishes to apprehend. Our knowledge of the external world is effected, then, by a likeness between the knower and the known; there must be in the senses "a likeness of the accidents of the sensible object, and in the intellect a likeness of the essence of the object understood." [21] *Our knowledge of the external world, therefore, is also always an image of our own being;* for every image in the mind expresses something about ourselves, and like our own being itself, is an indissoluble unity of spiritual and corporeal (sentient) principles.

This understanding of the character of knowledge indicates that, for Thomas, the natural world stands in a relation both to our human minds and to the mind of God. What has never in any way been brought to our notice does

[21] St. Thomas Aquinas, *Summa contra Gentiles,* trans. English Dominican Fathers (London: Burns Oates and Washbourne, 1929), V, p. 54. (Book IV, Chap. xi.)

not exist for us, but everything is present to God, and therefore has existence in him and received from him its nature or creatureliness. That all things have been creatively thought by God gives them truth and goodness and a lucidity which shines in us when we behold them. And if we object to the idea of truth being attributed to existence, when strictly it should belong only to thought, Thomas would readily understand this, but point out that the essential character of things is a manifestation of the thinking which devises and shapes and creates, and because things themselves are also thoughts within us, and receive their definition within our minds and therefore have the character of a word, they may honestly be called "true" in the way that one ordinarily calls what is thought "true."

So the truth of things, for Thomas, does not rest merely upon a recognition of things by our minds, but upon a relationship between our environment and our perceiving. It is peculiar to our surrounding world that its nature is acquired through our perceiving, and that its characteristics and its reality are shared and possessed by us in this way. In accepting this statement about the truth of things we must recognise that it refers to the essence and not to the existence of things, to their whatness (*Washeit,* quiddity) and not to the fact that they are "there"; it speaks of their qualities and characteristics, but not of the fact simply that they are to be encountered by us in space-time.

Our relationship with actually existing things is present before we begin to observe the world, and its development depends upon our initiative. In this respect we relate ourselves to things, while they are only passively related to our minds. Our relationship with the existence of things has its origin in the perceiving mind and not in the object.

But when we speak about the essence of things, the relationship is different. When we consider the essence—not the "that" but the "what"—of things, the relationship may be initiated from the side of the external world as well as from our perceiving minds. We recognise that things are potentially intelligible, and that their recognisableness awaits translation by us into knowledge. In this relationship our minds construct within themselves the forms of those external things which awaited our recognition, but in this process of upbuilding, and in response to our observation, the unexpected behaviour of things may well change our minds, redirect our thoughts or moderate their contents.

The aim of this relation to the essence of things, according to Thomas, is to establish an identity between the forms of external objects in our minds and the actual nature of the objects themselves, to create mental patterns which exactly correspond with the qualities and behavioural characteristics of the external world. The statement that "all that is, is true" means that everything without exception is related to the inwardness of a knowing mind, and must obviously rest upon this, that the knowing mind is oriented towards total reality and is bent upon finding accord and coming to an understanding with all that is. Things can be called true only when they are related to a perceiving mind which desires to understand them, for their truth lies in the conformity of the intellect with all the manifestations of their existence. Unlike the view which represents things as "the boundaries of men," the "truth of things" hides a mind directed towards their understanding; it envisages a field of relationships with the mind in the midst of the field; it sees the essences of things themselves possessed by the mind.

We do not fully apprehend the external world; we are

never able to turn its knowability completely into knowledge; some unknowableness remains. This is not due to the lack of lucidity in things, but to the limited ability of our minds to penetrate reality; yet the brilliance of things is inexhaustible by virtue of their being related to a perceiving mind. (This was before the Deism of the Enlightenment attributed to God a spatial transcendence which demolished the inwardness of things in him!) And here is Thomas' argument against the criticism that things do not possess objectivity in themselves, and that in order to become objects, things have to be related to a perceiving mind. The subject-object relations which develop with our growing awareness of things are not a creation of our minds but a datum, a condition which we encounter and accept, for things are actually objects in themselves; truth, in the sense of knowability, belongs to them. It is not that objective reality persists in unrelated isolation from a knowing mind, but that it does exist apart from our minds. The fact that things have a power to manifest existence, to reveal what they are, argues a relation with some perceiver: it argues that everything is "in God."

Nowadays, it will be said that we can surely think about the nature of objects without needing to consider that these natures are called into being by creative thought. It is, therefore, surprising to see the curious shadow of Aquinas' teaching about the truth of things falling across the structure of Jean-Paul Sartre's atheistic thinking. In *Existentialism and Humanism* Sartre points out that belief in God as creator carries the notion of a supernal artisan, so that the conception of man in the mind of God is comparable with that of any manufactured object in the mind of its maker, and that from this viewpoint, the essence of man precedes his historic existence.

But the atheistic existentialism which Sartre represents declares

with greater consistency that if God does not exist there is at least one being whose existence comes before its essence, a being which exists before it can be defined by any conception of it. That being is man . . . [who] first of all exists, encounters himself, surges up in the world—and defines himself after wards. . . . Thus there is no human nature because there is no God to have a conception of it.[22]

Though Sartre uses it negatively he begins with the assumption that things have an *essential* nature inasmuch as they are creatively thought. And the fact that things are creatively thought by the Creator is what Aquinas means in speaking of the truth of all existing things.

In our century, however, no one has shown greater interest in the relation between man and things than Edmund Husserl, particularly in his earlier writings.[23] He saw no reason to share Kant's distrust of experience or to mourn over the inaccessibility of things in themselves. He uses the word "phenomenon" as the Greeks did, for whom it meant "that which displays itself," though the display is for those who experience it. Everyday experience is of a certain *whatness* (*Washeit*) of things, and comprises their character in such a way that even when an object ceases to be physically present, its nature remains to be studied. Phenomena, then, are essences, and *represent* the external world, which exists in its own right. Against "unknowability" theories phenomena are objects of a particular kind of experience, namely of intuition; they are a datum of intui-

[22] (London: Methuen, 1948), pp. 27–28.
[23] *Logische Untersuchungen* and *Ideen zu einer reinen Phänomenologie und phänomenologischen Philosophie* (Halle: M. Niemeyer, 1913–22). *Ideen,* trans. W. R. Boyce Gibson (New York: Macmillan, 1931), under the title *Ideas.*

tive cognition, and as essences form the contents of our consciousness. The essential Being of the world can be known, and is known in every experience insofar as it has or imparts meaning. And if we wish to know how phenomena can simultaneously comprise both the qualities of objects perceived and the contents of our consciousness, Husserl says that every known object has the characteristic of experienceability:

What things are . . . they are as things of experience. Experience alone prescribes their meaning, and indeed when the concern is with factual things it is actual experience in its definitely ordered, empirical connections which does the prescribing.[24]

If this be so, it is nonsense to speak of anything which is not somehow experienced or known in some form of consciousness. The inexperienceable (not the inexperienced) simply does not exist. Every object—factual, actual, natural, imaginary or essential—is at least a potential object of experience of some kind. So Husserl does not deny that the external world enjoys a kind of existence in its own right, but to be known is to be experienced; and to be experienced means nothing less than to be in relation to an ego and its consciousness.

There are two realms of experience and an appropriate way of experiencing each of them; the two realms and the two ways of experiencing them are related. Natural experiencing is aware of a world spread out in space. Corporeal things, animals, objects, people are spatially distributed before us. They are not all in our vision, but we "know" that they are "there"; they are more or less familiar. And we recognise that we, too, are a part of this fact-world, which is

[24] *Ideas,* p. 88.

boundless in time and infinitely extended in space. We accept this world as being "out there" both for us and for everybody else; we do not think of it as dependent upon us but, rather, of ourselves as dependent upon it, especially as it restricts or helps our plans and actions.

But we are not always related to this fact-world alone; we can be occupied with numbers and the laws they represent. This arithmetical world may be present for our consciousness (and not on account of it), so long as we adopt the particular attitude which calls it into being. This world is not only a world of facts, but also of values.

In contrast with this, however, the experience of essences is immediate. It is the result of intuition. Natural experiencing, in and for itself, is inadequate and imperfect; without the intuitive experience of essences it would be meaningless. This knowledge of essences is "connected with," indeed is only possible in and through sense experience, yet it is apprehension of a different kind. Its descriptions belong to a time and space other than that of the objects it describes. Intuition refers to acts of consciousness in which the essences of things are "presented" to us. Our perceptions of the concrete world carry within them this insight into its meaning, and the natural world is what it is because of the realm of essences which constitute it.

Husserl objects to the contention that the "factual" is the only world. Those who hold this view say that even granting the possible existence of another world, it would not be experienceable or knowable, since all knowledge, conditioned as it is by our psychosomatic make-up, must always be restricted to the "natural" world. According to Husserl this empiricism rightly holds that all knowledge springs from experience, but wrongly contends for sense experience alone. He is convinced that

Genuine science and the genuine absence of prejudice peculiar to it demand, as a foundation of all proofs, judgements which as such are immediately valid, drawing their validity from originally given intuitions.[25]

In the course of perceiving the world, the contents of our perception are continually changing, yet the object we are looking at somehow remains the same. This is because its essence has been given through intuition. We do not, for example, see the whole of a tree at once, but we catch its meaning; in fact it need not be physically present, for a tree in a picture can still be enjoyed for its meaning. Mere perception as such does not constitute genuine experience; it lacks the meaning which pure consciousness supplies.

In addition to this, Husserl says that we experience the world by virtue of the intentional character of experiencing. Consciousness is more than consciousness of something (cf. William James); it points to objects and is intentionally related to them. The world of consciousness is a world of intentions. The distinction between objects vaguely apprehended and those upon which attention is focussed makes possible the difference between mere awareness and actual experiencing. In the latter the observer glances towards the object of his correlating consciousness and sees its essence or meaning, and not until this happens do objects become matters of genuine experience. This creative glance allows us to receive the meaning of objects through acts of intuiting, and it is in this sense, we may say, that we "constitute" the objects before us. The German noun *Meinung*, which

[25] *Ideas*, p. 36; cf. Max Planck's *Scientific Autobiography and Other Papers* (New York: Philosophical Library, 1949), p. 109: "When the pioneer in science sends forth the groping feelers of his thoughts, he must have a vivid intuitive imagination, for new ideas are not generated by deduction, but by an artistically creative imagination."

signifies "meaning" or "opinion," has the same stem as the verb *meinen*, "to intend," and Husserl takes a meaning to be an intention of the mind. Our part is to turn intentionally towards things; our turning supplies the basis of intuitive activity, which then makes it possible for objects to announce to us their essential qualities. Beyond Berkeley's dictum that "to be is to be perceived" Husserl maintains that it is the perceiver's intentional glance towards objects which gives them not their existence, but their essence: their depth of meaning and validity.

Realists in our time may define consciousness in terms of the brain or nervous system, and mind as the response of a physical organism to its environment. But for Husserl the mind is more than the "continuous feature" of our relationship with the world; it can act without reference to objects in time-space. And although the mind is not alien to nature, its capacity for intentional activity, its remembering, willing, imagining, inventing and creating, its possession of sense concepts, its dynamic character, make the realist descriptions of mind as "nothing in itself" extremely difficult.

According to Husserl's fundamental insight we are not simply objects in the world, nor is the world a mere thought in our minds; he does not say that matter is an illusion, nor that we generate the world out of thought, but that the inaccessible thing-in-itself and the independent ego have been superseded in a relationship in which human beings and the world make no sense apart from one another. His mutual concepts of "intuition" and "object" bridge the abyss between what appears in sensibility and the cause of its appearance, for they are not set side by side in virtue of a casual whim; their association, he says, is "compellingly commanded by the very nature of things." [26] Every possible object has its own ways of coming under a glance that presents, intuits, meets it essentially in its "bodily selfhood," and "lays hold" of it. What intuition grasps is "pure essence," and through the recognition of essences, the bestowal of meanings, man himself participates in a community of nature.[27]

Thus Husserl reinstates the world in its diversity, and denies the transcendent power of reason. Thinking is learning to see all over again, to be attentive, to focus consciousness; it is turning every idea and image into a privileged moment (Camus), and is justified inasmuch as it contributes to "an attitude for understanding."

At the beginning of this chapter appears a statement by Henri Bergson; the following comments upon it will serve both to conclude this discussion and to point towards matters of a similar character to be considered. When Bergson speaks about authentic philosophising there can be no mistaking the meaning of his statement. It does not mean that well-posed questions will bring the answers we were looking for, but rather that we invent the answers along with our questions. It is not a matter of there being a question in us and a response in things, or an external being to be discovered by an observing consciousness or a prying mind. The solution to our question is also in us, while the world outside us remains problematic. Something of the nature of the question passes into the answer. We do not need to go outside ourselves in order to reach things themselves. We are haunted by them from within. Our relation-

[26] *Ibid.*, p. 55.

[27] In a later chapter we shall note the development of this relationship by Husserl's disciple, Max Scheler.

ship with things is not frontal, like that of a spectator before a spectacle; it is a kind of complicity. When we speak of the essences of things, whatever they may be, *we* are *of* those essences. The qualities of objects are the qualities of people. Jean-Paul Sartre's words are not inappropriate here:

> To the extent that I appear to myself as *creating* objects by the sole relation of appropriation, these objects are myself. . . . The totality of my possessions reflects the totality of my being. I *am* what I have. It is I myself which I touch in this cup, in this trinket. This mountain which I climb is myself to the extent that I conquer it; and when I am at its summit which I have achieved at the cost of this same effort, when I attain this magnificent view of the valley and the surrounding peaks, then I *am* the view; the panorama is myself dilated to the horizon, for it exists only through me, only for me.[28]

This genitive relation means that our experience of things, the sense data we perceive, are variants of ourselves, and are symbolic of our life. Matter-in-itself is not interior to us; it can only be a question of matter perceived by us. The relationship we are attempting to trace is, therefore, simply a story of ourselves which we tell ourselves. It is a natural myth by which we express our ability to get along with the world. We are not this stone, but when we look at it, it awakens resonances in our perceptive apparatus. Our perception seems to come from it, but our seeing and handling of the stone promotes it to conscious existence in ourselves. We recover this mute thing which, from the time it enters our life, begins to unfold its implicit being; and its essence is created by us in our relationship towards it.

[28] *Being and Nothingness* (New York: Philosophical Library, 1956), pp. 590–91.

5

The Thinking Earth

We have the ideas of matter and thinking, but possibly shall never be able to know whether any material being thinks or no; it being impossible for us, by contemplation of our own ideas, to discover whether Omnipotency has not given to some systems of matter, fitly disposed a power to perceive and think, or else joined and fixed to matter, so disposed, a thinking immaterial substance; it being, in respect of our notions, not much more remote from our comprehension to conceive that God can, if he pleases, superadd to matter a faculty of thinking, than that he should superadd to it another substance with a faculty of thinking.

John Locke [1]

Had I been present at the birth of this planet I would probably not have believed on the word of an Archangel that the blazing mass, the incandescent whirlpool there before our eyes at a temperature of fifty million degrees would presently set about the establishment of empires and civilizations, that it was on its way to produce Greek art and Italian painting.

W. Macneile Dixon [2]

IN THE THIRTEENTH CENTURY Duns Scotus asked, Can matter think? [3] John Locke suggested, though without great concern, that for all we know God might have given the power of thinking to a purely material thing. It was left to Leibniz to take the suggestion seriously. Provoked by

[1] *Essay concerning Human Understanding,* Book IV, Chap. III, 6.

[2] *The Human Situation:* Gifford Lectures, 1935–37 (London: E. Arnold, 1937), paraphrase of a passage on p. 127.

[3] K. Marx and F. Engels, quoted in *The Holy Family* (Moscow: Foreign Languages Publishing House, 1956), p. 172.

92

dissatisfaction with Descartes's extended substance and the subsequent reduction of matter to a phantomlike quality during eighteenth-century philosophical discussion, Leibniz sought to bridge the separating distance between the theoretical understanding of matter and men's practical experience of it, with a new concept of the nature of the world. Believing that the soul mirrors the universe, and that the necessities of thought reflect and determine the nature of things, he stated that substance is not an aggregate of parts such as the idea of spread-outness seemed to necessitate, but that it is a centre of force. There is nothing dead in nature. Everything in it is sentient and animated. Every bit of matter is a world of creatures, souls, entelechies, of an infinity of kinds.

Without analysing the sensible properties of matter, but rather by looking into the continuously active, self-organising and self-determining centre of energy which was himself, Leibniz formed by analogy a general idea of substance. Every substance, or created monad, is a "self-sufficiency" (αὐτάρκεια) which makes each a source of its own internal activities.[4] Each monad is unique, true to its individual character, and a microcosm independent of anything outside itself for its own development. Each monad is an immaterial active unit of "thought" life which in multiplicity, however, constitutes the basis of all spiritual and physical reality.

Each monad expresses a particular phase of the universe, and because each in itself is a "perpetual mirror of the universe"[5] it also reflects what is common to all. This reflec-

[4] *The Monadology of Leibniz,* introduced by H. W. Carr (Los Angeles: University of California, 1930), Section 18, p. 56.

[5] *Ibid.,* Section 56, pp. 98–99.

93

tive ability makes each monad an integral part of the whole and maintains the harmony of all. Differences of perceptual activity in monads vary by infinitely small gradations from the confused thought of "unconscious" things to the clarity of conscious beings. Continuous series of monads, ranging from lowest to highest in gradual development, mean that matter and spirit are not divided; where there was thought to be a cleft between organic and inorganic, continuity prevails; between the blind working of force in material things and the creative working of mind in human beings lies no essential difference. The highest monads comprising the soul, surrounded by innumerable monads of lower orders forming a body, together make a living being.

In this way Leibniz healed the breach between body and mind, and gave to material substance a real and necessary place in the structure of human beings, and set man firmly once again within the wholeness of the world. For although each monad is a world apart, its development is in correspondence with the changes in all other monads in accordance with a pre-established harmony.

Nietzsche was greatly indebted to Leibniz, the depth of whose "incomparable insight," he said, "has not as yet been exhausted." [6] The source of this indebtedness lies in part at those points in the monadology which suggest that each monad is a centre of energy, that continuous series of monads bridge the apparently qualitative difference between material things and the human mind, and that the monad, therefore, constitutes the basis of all physical and spiritual reality.

These characteristics have a formative influence upon Nietzsche's concept of the Will to Power which expresses

[6] *Joyful Wisdom*, X (New York: Russell & Russell, 1964), p. 305.

finally the notion of creativity. His choice of the concept was the outcome of arduous searching rather than sudden illumination. He had set aside "the will to live"—inasmuch as we are alive; "the will to happiness" seemed to exclude the acceptance of unhappiness—a necessary ingredient of happiness in this world. "The will to health" or "wholeness" more closely approximated to his feeling for life, yet did not suffice. Man's will is not simply a matter of growth, but of creativity. All self-creation is a prelude to creating.

The will to power defines man's deepest self: the primary impulse out of which our instincts have originated, the power which triumphs over inward division and seeks ever greater unities, the power which our instincts are appointed to serve, is a will to create. Intellect, will, sentiments—all depend upon our valuations. These valuations correspond to our instincts and their conditions of existence. Our instincts are reducible to the will to power. This is the ultimate fact, the basic character of the entire animate and inanimate world, so that whatever action manifests itself, it is of the same kind as human action.

Nietzsche conceived of it as his task to "translate man back into nature," [7] to overcome all those enticements to believe human origins to be other than those of the rest of nature. He asks us to assume that nothing is "given" as real except our world of desires and passions, that we cannot rise or sink to any other kind of "reality" save that of our drives ("for thinking is only a relation of these impulses to one another"). May we not then ask the question, he continues, whether this datum does not suffice for understanding the so-called mechanistic or material world as well?

Assuming that we managed to explain the whole of our

[7] *Beyond Good and Evil,* XII (New York: Russell & Russell, 1964), pp. 179–81.

instinctive life as a development of one basic form of will (the "Will to Power," as Nietzsche held), it would then be justifiable to define all effective energy, unequivocally, as will to power. "The world seen from within, the world designated and defined according to its 'intelligible character'—this world would be *Will to Power* and nothing else." [8]

Such a conjecture must arouse animosity in many scientific minds, but Nietzsche argued that "It is an illusion to suppose that something is known when all we have is a mathematical formula of what has happened: it is only *characterised, described;* no more!" [9] In addition to this, and with increasing emphasis, scientists are insisting upon a continuity between the inorganic, the organic and the human worlds. If, therefore, the postulate of a basic tendency towards the acquisition of power fits the facts of human nature, and enables us to predict new facts, there is no reason to suspect that it may not fulfil the same role in respect of the rest of nature.

Nietzsche suggested that science had set out with the intention of tracing the unknown back to the known, but had ended by tracing the known back to the unknown. However, "a force of which we cannot form any idea, is an empty word, and ought to have no civic rights in the city of science": [10] so that

The triumphant concept "energy" with which our physicists created God and the world, needs yet to be completed: it must be given an inner will which I characterise as the 'Will to

[8] *Ibid.,* p. 52.

[9] *The Will to Power* in *The Complete Works of Friedrich Nietzsche,* ed. Oscar Levy (New York: Russell & Russell, 1964), XV, p. 114.

[10] *Ibid.,* p. 111.

Power'. . . . There is no help for it, all movements, all 'appearances', all 'laws' must be understood as *symptoms* of an inner phenomenon, and the analogy of man must be used for this purpose.[11]

This is Nietzsche's hypothesis, which he proceeded to test in relation to the world of events, of persons and things. He does not regard the material world as an illusion; its multiplicity of phenomena is not merely a product of our minds; other people's wills are as real as our own; but there are not two kinds of substance as Descartes had suggested. The ultimate constituents of the world are dynamic, so that the true being of everything consists in its action. Nothing acts regularly; nothing follows a rule, the fact that something is as it is, strong or weak, is not the result of obedience to a rule. The reality about which all phenomena move is a matter of degrees of resistance and superior power. Things are calculable because they cannot possibly be otherwise than they are; "a quantum of power is characterized by the effect it produces and the influence it resists." [12] And although a state of indifference is thinkable in itself, it is entirely lacking. A quantum of power is "essentially a will to violence and a will to defend one's self against violence. It is not self-preservation: every atom exercises its influence over the whole of existence—it is thought out of existence if one thinks this radiation of will-power away." [13] So the ultimate constituents of the world are "dynamic quanta, in a relation of tension to all other dynamic quanta: the essence of which resides in their relation to all other quanta,

[11] *Ibid.*, p. 110.
[12] *Ibid.*, pp. 117–18.
[13] *Ibid.*, p. 118.

in their 'influence' upon the latter." [14] If, then, the primary constituent of matter is nothing that acts, but activity itself, we must banish the thought of anything merely passive in the universe.

Descartes's two substances must be excluded; indeed, the idea of substance, says Nietzsche, is an outcome of the concept "subject":

We distinguish ourselves, the agents, from the action, and everywhere we make use of this scheme—we try to discover an agent behind every phenomenon. We have *misunderstood* a feeling of power, tension, resistance, a muscular feeling, which is already the beginning of the action, and posited it as a cause; or we have to understand the will to do this or that, as a cause, because the action follows from it.[15]

We ourselves have no existence apart from the sum-total of our activities, conscious and unconscious; no more has anything else; for "matter" is simply an abstraction for a dynamic event.

When, therefore, it is understood that the "subject" is nothing that *acts,* but is only a thing of fancy, then things-in-themselves also vanish; for only with the subject as model did we invent *thingness.* In the final analysis the "thing-in-itself" is a conception of the "subject-in-itself," and if we abandon the idea of the acting subject, we also abandon the object acted upon; the idea of "substance" disappears, and so does "materiality."

This concept of the world as sheer Will to Power is not used by Nietzsche to deny sensory data, but rather to establish the nature of subject-object relations. We do not stand over against nature as detached, dispassionate observers of

[14] *Ibid.,* p. 120.
[15] *Ibid.,* p. 56.

phenomena unconnected with ourselves. All our observations bear the stamp of action and interaction. Knowing means placing ourselves in relation with something, modifying it and being modified by it, so that the ordering of the objective world is a systematising of relations with it—and therefore a simultaneous ordering of ourselves!

The will to truth is a process of *establishing* things: it is a process of making things true and lasting. . . . 'truth' is not something which is present and which has to be found and discovered; it is something *which has to be created* and which *gives* its name *to a process,* or, better still, to the will to overpower. . . . to introduce truth is . . . an active determining —it is not a process of becoming conscious of something in itself as fixed and determined. It is merely a word for 'The Will to Power'.[16]

On the basis of this description of the dynamic unity of the world and of the determining character of its fundamental reality, the Will to Power, Nietzsche enquires whether it is not permissible to accept the world as equal in reality-stature to our passions? Must we not understand it as a more primitive form of the world of passions in which everything, still contained in a powerful unison, later branches off and develops in the organic processes? And he reaches the point where these experimental questions give way to a demand that we understand the material world as a primary form of life.[17]

The concept of "matter" has today given way to that of "energy." Inert substance itself is understood in terms of equilibria of torrents of movement, and its very continuity

---

[16] *Ibid.,* pp. 60–61.

[17] *Beyond Good and Evil,* XII (New York: Russell & Russell, 1964), pp. 51–52.

as a continuity of change. Form and substance are one; they are patterns of behaviour; and this is so wherever matter is—in rock, or tree, or man. But this dynamic equilibrium, or balanced chaos of forces, Nietzsche regards as an incomplete appraisal of the nature of the world which, on the analogy of man, must have an inwardness, an intelligible character, and must be seen as discriminating, determining "Will to Power."

The insight of Nietzsche's two contemporaries, Karl Marx and Friedrich Engels, into the living nature of matter seems to have been overlooked or ignored both by their detractors and by their less distinguished successors. But they, too, drew inspiration from the Greek cosmologists, particularly from Heraclitus, whom Engels regarded as one of the precursors of dialectical materialism. He writes:

When we reflect on nature, or the history of mankind, or on our own intellectual activity, the first picture presented to us is of an endless maze of relations and interactions, in which nothing remains what, where, and as it was, but everything moves, changes, comes into being and passes out of existence. This primitive, naive, yet intrinsically correct conception of the world was that of ancient Greek philosophy, and was first clearly formulated by Heraclitus: everything is in *flux*, is constantly changing, constantly coming into being and passing away.[18]

In considering the nature of matter, Marx returns to Francis Bacon and Bacon's contemporary, Jakob Boehme, in order to endorse their views with approbation:

The first and most important of the inherent qualities of *matter* is *motion,* not only *mechanical* and *mathematical* movement, but still more *impulse, vital life-spirit, tension,* or to use Jacob

[18] *Landmarks of Scientific Socialism* (*Anti-Dühring*), (Chicago: C. H. Kerr, 1907), pp. 26–27.

Boehme's expression, the throes (Qual) of matter. The primary forms of matter are the living, individualizing *forces of being* inherent in it and producing the distinctions between the species.[19]

In Francis Bacon, materialism's "first creator," there emerges a view of the world which is filled with the promise of development: "Matter smiled at man with poetical, sensuous brightness." It was Hobbes who, according to Marx, systematised Bacon's materialism, emphasised mechanical motion over against physical motion, so that materialism became hostile to humanity.

In the "Dialectics of Nature" Engels describes the human mind as "the highest product of organic matter," and subsequently says:

The motion of matter is not merely crude mechanical motion, mere change of place, it is heat and light, electric and magnetic tension, chemical combination and dissociation, life and, finally, consciousness.[20]

The materialism of Marx and Engels is basically an assertion of the priority of matter, but it is never a denial of the reality of mind. Matter is not inert, but lively, and when not actually imbued with physical life as we experience it, then still pregnant with life. Once the ideally favourable conditions are present, then matter, hitherto characterised by "mechanical and mathematical movement" bursts into life and bestows living creatures upon the world.

How this qualitative leap occurs is still unexplained, yet the further knowledge advances the less clear becomes the

[19] *The Holy Family* (Moscow: Foreign Languages Publishing House, 1956), p. 172.

[20] *On Religion* (Moscow: Foreign Languages Publishing House, 1956), p. 171.

dividing line between organic and inorganic,[21] though distinctions between them are patent and undeniable. These distinctions, however, are not contradictory, according to Engels, who pointed out that

the more men feel and know themselves to be one with nature . . . the more impossible will be the senseless and anti-natural idea of a contradiction between mind and matter, man and nature, soul and body.[22]

The vision which Marx and Engels shared of an earthly paradise to be realised with inexorable certainty did not, therefore, depend upon the will or the power of proletarian man, but upon these lively forces which they believed to be inherent in the material world: energies which had always been working towards the apocalyptic denouement of which they both dreamed. And it was on the basis of this *dialectical* materialism and man's vital relationship with the earth that Marx propounded his view which demanded that the empirical world be so arranged that, within it, man might experience and accustom himself to what is really human, and become aware of himself as man. "If man is shaped by

[21] cf. Karl Heim, *The transformation of the Scientific World View* (London: SCM Press, 1953), pp. 207 ff, cites a number of striking discoveries on this frontier. For example (p. 211), the distinction between organic and inorganic self-nurture is called into question at the point where crystals grow: "Crystals do not grow simply by external addition or deposits of new substance which resembles the old. At the surface of the crystal there is a delicate shell, distinct from the interior of the crystal. This 'crystal membrane' is so arranged that it is able to select, transform, attach to itself and assimilate material from the environment. Once the crystal membrane has fulfilled its task, it retires from the scene, and a new surface is extruded in place of the old one. This takes over the 'physiological function' performed by its predecessor. . . . The crystal membrane includes within its capacity for assimilation the power to transform and adapt itself when there is a change in the flow of nourishment in its vicinity."

[22] "Dialectics of Nature," *On Religion*, p. 188.

his surroundings, his surroundings must be made human." [23]

The apparent restriction of the phenomenon of consciousness to the higher forms of life has often served science as an excuse for eliminating consciousness from its models of the universe. Inwardness, as interior life, was regarded as an exception. But an evolutionary appraisal of the natural world, and the logic based upon it, seem to demand that minds should have evolved as well as bodies, and that accordingly mindlike properties must be present throughout the universe. In every region of time and space, coextensive with the sensible properties of things, there must also be an inwardness of things.

Leibniz, Nietzsche, Marx and Engels have been grouped together here as representatives of a particular family of ideas concerning the stuff of the universe; to their number we should add Bergson, who also speaks of a "presentiment" and of an "imitation" of memory in matter. He treats of consciousness as a substance spread out through the universe, which in rudimentary organisms is "compressed in a kind of vice" and which in more differentiated organisms is allowed to develop.[24]

At this point, to allay suspicion that the argument is drifting towards panpsychism, or that the writer is unaware of this, it must be said that if the enquiry were a turning back to look for our ancestry in things, the temptation might

[23] *The Holy Family*, p. 176.

[24] Henri Bergson, *Matter and Memory* (New York: Macmillan, 1912), p. 313: "No doubt also the material universe itself, defined as the totality of images, is a kind of consciousness." Mention of Bergson must be accompanied also by two Gifford lecturers from the English-speaking world: Samuel Alexander in *Space, Time and Deity* (London: Macmillan, 1920) and C. Lloyd Morgan in *Emergent Evolution,* and *Life, Mind and Spirit* (New York: Henry Holt, 1923 and 1925 respectively) reveal their kinship with Bergson.

arise to project souls into things. But we are not attempting to return to origins. We are simply searching for a relationship of our persons with things, here and now, and to grant them "inwardness" is not to invest them with souls. The essential factor in our kind of thinking is the assimilation of the unfamiliar, the harmonising of new material with old schemes; "thinking" in a primitive (inorganic) state, according to Nietzsche, for example, "means to *persevere in forms,* as in the case of the crystal." [25]

This thought of the inwardness of things gradually loses its strangeness in the realisation that the categories into which nature is divided for man's convenience and investigation have no counterparts in reality. The division of matter into dead and living forms, useful for distinguishing extreme cases, becomes increasingly inappropriate for assessing the broad intervening hierarchy of being.

In his essay entitled "Science and Ethics," J. B. S. Haldane wrote:

We do not find obvious evidence of life or mind in so-called inert matter, and we naturally study them most easily where they are most completely manifested; but if the scientific point of view is correct, we shall ultimately find them, at least in rudimentary forms, all through the universe.[26]

His suggestion is being nurtured by subsequent evidence. The ability to nourish itself and to grow, the ability to receive stimuli and to react to them, have long been re-

[25] *The Will to Power* in Levy, *op. cit.,* XIV, pp. 22 (cf. reference to crsytals by Karl Heim, quoted in n. 21 on p. 102).

[26] *Conway Memorial Lecture* (Watts: London, 1928), p. 34. Cf. also a parallel statement by Julian Huxley in his introduction to Pierre Teilhard de Chardin's *The Phenomenon of Man* (London: Collins, 1959), p. 16. ". . . we must infer the presence of potential mind in all material systems, by backward extrapolation from the human phase to the biological, and from the biological to the inorganic."

104

garded as functions which differentiated the living cell from "dead" material. Reports show that it becomes increasingly clear that these three life-functions are also found, in other forms and on lower levels, in the elementary particles of inorganic matter. The more deeply and finely researchers probe into the delicate structure of materials (leptology) and the mysterious agitation of particles "within the wholeness of individuals which make up so-called dead stuff," the more sharply are they confronted with the question: Where is the frontier at which inert matter ceases and organic life begins? and, Is there a complete antithesis between "dead" and "living"? [27] These questions recall the comfortless assurance offered by P. B. Medawar to those who fear the possibility of not being actually dead when certified to be so: "As dead as mutton," he submits, is a phrase superannuated by the march of time, "and those whose most pressing fear it is that they will be lowered living into their graves can have their doubts resolved: they will be." [28]

The frontiers of the animate world press ever more deeply into the realms of the inanimate. C. F. von Weizsäcker, in his book *The World View of Physics,* examines one of his personal possessions: an Icelandic calcite crystal.[29] He describes what a physicist or geologist would say about it, then considers its "personal" qualities; that is to say, the "place" or "meaning" of the crystal within his own personal history or lifetime.

The size and purity of the crystal speak of far-off geological circumstances attendant upon its formation. The crystal has a determinate weight—the sum of the weights of its atomic nuclei. It is a solid body, chemically analysable and,

[27] Cf. Karl Heim, *op. cit.,* p. 210.
[28] *The Uniqueness of the Individual* (London: Methuen, 1957), p. 27.
[29] (London: Routledge & Kegan Paul, 1952), pp. 13 ff.

because its atoms are regularly bound together in space, exhibits a regular crystalline form. It is transparent but double-refracting—a single line observed through it appears double. Its transparency is connected with its inability to conduct electricity. These and other sensory observations can all be reduced to atomic processes. Indeed, the crystal could be "smashed to atoms," and the atoms—which would then be neither calcite nor crystal—might be further analysed into constituents no longer perceptible to the senses.

Von Weizsäcker then asks whether anything is lacking in this picture, or if the picture itself is restricted to a segment of reality. In taking the crystal from its drawer he had been reminded of the teacher who brought it back from Iceland for him, and the recollection had stirred his emotions. The power of the crystal to stir him emotionally was not one of its physical properties, and might even be dismissed as a "subjective process" in the observer. But who has decreed that these subjective realities are less important for a person who wants to make himself a true picture of the world? Methods of physical enquiry are concerned with phenomena accessible to all. What justification is there, however, for considering that what is accessible to all is more real than that which is accessible to one person only? A comfortable way of disposing of this problem is to say that there are two equally justifiable "aspects" under which nature may be regarded: the subjective and the objective. But one of the major concerns of our present enquiry, and the important problem posed by von Weizsäcker himself, is contained in the fact that these two "aspects" stand in an inner and indivisible relationship to one another.

How do I really know that my psychological relation to this crystal does not belong to it as an objective property—that is, one perceptible to other people? Is it perhaps only that our sense for the objective but unconscious relations between the physical and the mental is too little developed? Are there perhaps in these relationships objectively existent basic structures to which our conscious subjective feelings are related as the individual properties of this one fragment of crystal are to its general property of being calcite crystal? [30]

In order to rescue from the realm of fancy these questions of the presence in matter of structures with emotion-rousing capacity, von Weizsäcker recalls men's earlier belief in the magical properties of precious stones: a belief which, by inference, indicates a quality in the crystal not verifiable to physics. From a physical world-view can a judgement of "superstition" be passed upon this belief? Surely not. If such effects do not occur within a physical world-view it is because it consciously ignores their possibility in advance. But what respectable physicist would deny the reality of such effects if they were exhibited to him in practise? The completeness of the presuppositions on which contemporary physics is constructed cannot be demonstrated, and we must therefore say that the physical world-view leaves room, in principle, for such effects, inasmuch as it partakes of the incompleteness of experience.

In the course of our thinking we concluded that our knowledge of the external world was always also an image of ourselves, that sensory data awakened resonances in our perceptive apparatus, and that our seeing and handling of objects promoted them to conscious existence within us where they unfold their implicit being. In other words, their essence is created in our relationship with them, and partakes of our own awareness of life. The essence of the crystal penetrates the life of the observer in accordance with the degree of his openness to its existence, and by the

[30] *Ibid.*, p. 17.

same token his inattention or ignorance encapsules it within its own spatial dimensions, leaving the observer both less aware of the life which surrounds him and less conscious of the potentiality and dimensions of his own person.

If, then, every image in the mind expresses something about ourselves, and, like us, is an indissoluble unity of mind and body, that is to say, of mental and sensory principles, then the people upon whose thoughts about the nature of the earth we have been commenting, were exposing to the physical world qualities of personality other than those which discursive reason allows. They were attempting to recognise the world more "humanly"—as Herder expressed it—and acknowledged that the story of the earth is the story of man. The furnace of molten rocks and metals, the rotating earth, they understood as yielding thoughts and values; they recognised that our planet had become a place of thinking, of "right" and "wrong," and that it had become human, a familial assembly, a community of related beings and things.

6

Language and Things

The 'universe', that is the whole mass of all things that are, is corporeal, that is to say body, and hath the dimensions of magnitude, namely length, breadth, and depth; also every part of body is likewise body and hath the like dimensions, and consequently every part of the universe is body, and that which is not body is no part of the universe; and, because the universe is all, that which is no part of it is 'nothing', and consequently 'nowhere'.

Thomas Hobbes [1]

Our choice of language is a matter of truth or error, of right or wrong,—of life or death.

Michael Polanyi [2]

IT IS NOT UNCOMMON for writers on the subject of "science and religion" to state in antithetical terms those views of the world held by each discipline. It is said, for example, that the moment we look at something "purely scientifically" we are alienated from it; the world becomes a huge *res extensa,* and objects become literally *Gegenstände,* things which stand over against us. Opposed to this scientific "view" of the world there is a nonscientific, intuitive relationship which argues an intimacy and a sense of belonging that scientific enquiry seeks to avoid. This kind of relationship to nature once shared by multitudes, has gradually become

[1] *Leviathan* (London: Routledge & Kegan Paul, 1886), Chap. xlvi, p. 471.

[2] *Personal Knowledge* (Chicago: University of Chicago Press, 1958), p. 113.

limited to poetic and artistic experience, and to some forms of mysticism. This contrast between the two attitudes to the world of things is summed up by saying that the scientist elucidates an object of nature as it *exists,* while the poet and the aesthete affirm its *essence.*

But what does an examination of the relationship between these two views of the world reveal? The limited kinds of human experiencing with which science associated itself may have encouraged the incompatibility already suggested. Forgetfulness that every science of nature depends upon presuppositions about nature which cannot be established by the methods of science itself, and the mingling of changing appraisals of the universe with confidence in the changeless "objectivity" of the experiencing self, are factors which have helped to create the antithesis between religious and scientific aspects of life. Yet scientists are not neutral observers of phenomena, and do not register sensory impressions without bias. Scientific investigation does not occur without committedness to some concept of value, so that freedom and neutrality in this sense are delusions of the conscious mind. We observe the world through eyes of our own personal history!

Consider Thomas Hobbes's statement at the head of this chapter, to the effect that the universe is entirely "material." As a statement about the nature of the world it must lose some of its efficacy immediately we recall that we have no knowledge of what the world is in itself, or of what "matter" may be, and that what we say about it describes our relationship with the world. If Hobbes's statement carries conviction in our minds, is its convincing quality different from that of an incantation? Does the statement not point to its author's attitude of mind? May its "meaning" perhaps be found in the emotions which it symbolises?

In his essay on Thomas Hobbes, Basil Willey suggests that "very nearly every statement of Hobbes can be reduced either to hatred and contempt of schoolmen and clerics, or to fear of civil war and love of ordered living in a stable commonwealth." [3] He also suggests that Hobbes's word about the materiality of the universe may have sprung from a plane of consciousness slanted in the following way:

Fear and reverence Nature no longer; she is no mystery, for she 'worketh by motion', and Geometry, which is the mother of the sciences, and indeed the only science God has yet vouchsafed to us—Geometry can chart these motions. Feel, then, as if you lived in a world which can be measured, weighed and mastered; and confront it with due audacity.[4]

Every man's understanding of the world is coloured by his predilections and experiences. While mathematicians visualise the world in terms of number, Christians may regard nature as a symbol of God; in a context of despair the world displays its indifference to man and his works; in the hour of triumph nature's blessings seem to rest upon mechanical power or brute force. How can nature or the world be interpreted except through our personal histories?

> . . . as is your sort of mind
> So is your sort of search: [5]

and is not every kind of knowledge not merely a "view," but a living relationship? The scientific view of the world is a particular and lively relationship of man with nature.

To illustrate two kinds of relationship with nature we

[3] *The Seventeenth Century Background* (London: Chatto and Windus, 1934), p. 95.

[4] *Ibid.*, p. 95.

[5] Robert Browning, "Easter Day," in *The Complete Poetic and Dramatic Works* (Boston and New York: Houghton-Mifflin, 1895), p. 328. Cf. E. Mounier's *Personalism* (London: Routledge & Kegan Paul, 1952), p. xx: "The person is a centre of reorientation of the objective universe."

may say that a study of Albrecht Dürer's picture of the rabbit will not make superfluous a course in zoology, nor will the observations of zoology concerning the phenomenon "rabbit" amount to the insight conveyed by the artist's representation. Neither the analytical relationship of the scientist nor the aesthete's feeling for life can be designated "true" or "false;" each relationship expresses a kind of participation in life. Reason demands systematised accounts of phenomena; the total man wishes to see the world as a whole; yet the distinctiveness of these attitudes tends to hide their mutuality and inseparability.

Nietzsche protested vividly that

We are not objectifying and registering apparatuses with cold entrails, it makes the most material difference whether a thinker is personally related to his problems, having his fate, his need, and his highest happiness bound together in the relationship, or only impersonally, in which case the problems are only grasped with the tentacles of coldly prying thinking. We must share with our thoughts all that we have in us of blood, heart, ardour, joy, passion, pang, conscience, fate and fatality.[6]

The importance of Nietzsche's protest against the omission of "personal" qualities in our efforts to understand the world is reinforced by Martin Buber, who also envisages two relationships—the scientific and the existential—as mutually enfolded. In *I and Thou* he contemplates a tree and the variety of ways in which it might be analysed. In those relationships which concern colour and movement, structure and constitution, law and number, the tree remains an object occupying space. But given "both will and grace" it can happen that a man becomes bound up in a different relation which, far from excluding the earlier

[6] *Joyful Wisdom,* X (New York: Russell & Russell, 1964), p. 6.

analyses, unites them indivisibly in this event. "Everything belonging to the tree is in this: its form and structure, its colours and chemical composition, its intercourse with the elements and with the stars, are all present in a single whole." [7]

This relation between man and tree is mutual, says Buber, though we are not to infer from this that the tree has consciousness similar to our own,[8] but rather that the essence of the tree, the tree itself, stands forth only within a willing and gracious relation with man, and will not bear analysis without disintegration. And Buber carefully affirms that the earlier scientific analyses are contained within the existential encounter, and that far from destroying the virtue of the experience, they inform it; so that one kind of experiencing is here enfolded within another, and an existential relationship with the world embraces scientific relationships without destroying or denying their validity.

In our engagement with life it is with words that we forge ideas, create the essences of things, and determine their nature in respect of our needs and interests. Words express a creative will by which a thing receives a name, and in this act of appellation we take possession of the world both physically and intellectually, and draw it into the orbit of our knowledge and influence. So then, language is a depository of human experience which holds man's abstract conception of the world and of life. Upon this storehouse of experience we all draw, for in order to think we begin with

[7] *I and Thou* (Edinburgh: T. & T. Clark, 1942), pp. 7–8.

[8] Cf. Miguel de Unamuno, *The Tragic Sense of Life* (New York: Dover, 1954), p. 150: "The feeling that Nature is a society has taken hold of me hundreds of times in walking through the woods, possessed with a sense of solidarity with the oaks, a sense of their dim awareness of my presence."

what our predecessors thought and preserved in linguistic form.

While the existence of things is a mystery and a datum, their essence, established within human relationships, reflect man's attitude towards the physical world. "Nature" reflects man's life, and as his self-awareness changes so does his awareness of the world. This awareness may be described. We may *speak* about it. Inasmuch as there is no thought without language, though there may be a frustrated intention of thinking, our relationship with things and the mutual interacting of essences discloses the importance of language in the dialogue of being which is our life. Our descriptions of things are not merely faithful images of what we have realised about the external world, but words are themselves the means whereby the external world acquires inwardness within us and receives its nature. Although language and sensibility may sometimes limit our participation in the being of the world, we incorporate them in the essences of things in such a way that although we do not say that things are only what we perceive by sense and describe in language, we do recognise sensory data and verbal description to be the elements by which essences appear.[9] The importance laid upon linguistic analysis in contemporary philosophy reflects this formative power of words: they are the "flesh of concepts" (Unamuno), and constitute the basis of creative action. In this sense we may speak of poetry, "the mother-tongue of humanity" (J. G. Hamann), aspiring to penetrate to the heart of things, to speak of their nature, and so to create things; for ποιεῖν is to produce or

[9] In discussing language and its relation to things it is not possible to reopen the matter of nonverbal communication (pp. 57–58) or that of the wisdom of the body (pp. 50–51), both of which imply the kind of knowledge that Michael Polanyi designates as "tacit."

to bring into existence. Poetry creates as it speaks, man gives himself to things and is shaped by what he gives, so that poetry is a kind of fusion of man with things: it objectifies man and at the same time subjectifies things.

From the viewpoint of logic we reckon that our minds form concepts by abstracting from things their differences, retaining their similarities, and reflecting upon these in order to group them into families of objects in our minds. Things are then recognised by certain essential properties which appear to be common to other members of their class. But how are differences and similarities noted prior to language? What are the rules for naming things? Why do we collect particular impressions into a class and denote them by a word? What makes language select from the stream of impressions just certain reflected lights to which it gives special significance? Logic itself cannot answer this last question, for the choice is determined partly by objects themselves, partly by existing language, and partly by the observer's stamp of mind: that is to say, by his personal needs and interests.

In a scientific relation to life men's minds are directed towards abolishing the uniqueness of actual events by relating them to other happenings. We gather things out of their isolation into a system; the mind is bent upon overcoming the singularity of occurrences in order to "grasp" them within the widest possible context, or to recognise them under a general idea as instances within a series. This discursive kind of thinking starts with a particular experience, and runs through a history of partly similar experiences in order to give character, a place, and some intellectual meaning to the event with which it is immediately confronted. Such theoretical knowledge, however, belongs to a stratum of logic which in turn rests upon a stratum of language. In order to be understood, phenomena must first be named, for our theoretical learning begins in a world already formed by language. The scientist, the historian and the philosopher live with the elements of their disciplines as language presents them; so although logical theory traces concepts back to processes of abstracting and selecting common properties from a variety of data, the problem of language is that of positing the properties themselves.

We have to notice the properties of things before we can denote them with words, and the observations which underlie speech and language betoken a peculiar spiritual character: that is to say, differences of speech or language are due to variations of inner perspective, and in each instance presuppose a special way of conceiving of and apprehending the world.

The idea that names and essences bear a necessary and internal relation to each other, that a name does not merely denote, but actually *is* the essence of its object, that there is a latent identity between names and essences, is one of the fundamental assumptions of mythopoeic thinking.[10] Whereas *logical* thinking pursues its discursive way, comparing the nature of one experience with many, setting it within a total explanation of the world, and by means of symbols establishing a relationship between a particular occurrence and a concept of unity, *mythical* thinking is captivated by immediate appearances, focusses all its powers upon a single point, is completely absorbed and "possessed" by it. Mythical thinking does not contemplate

[10] For definitions of two types of thinking I am indebted to Ernst Cassirer's *Language and Myth* (New York: Dover, 1946) and to Henri Frankfort's *Before Philosophy* (London: Penguin, 1949).

external reality; it neither compares nor relates it to anything else. One object or occasion in the outer world simply overcomes its beholder, who is caught up in a tension and held there by fear or hope, by terror or a sense of fulfilment.

Hermann Usener used this contrast in trying to understand how a religious conception of the world developed. He explained that when the excitement of mythic thinking abated, the person involved then invested the object or occasion in the external world with his own personal condition, and that the excitement thus objectified confronted him as a "momentary god," *ein Augenblicksgott,* or as a δαίμων.[11]

Usener held that, similarly, the formation of language belonged not to reflection but to spiritual excitement, not to clearheaded comparisons but to dynamic processes yielding sounds out of their own native strength: the inner tension of the occasion resolving itself into an outer form of myth or speech. As "momentary gods" transcend the unique moment of their birth and the memory of their original meaning, to live independent lives, so the uttered sounds of language exhibit a similar tendency to permanent existence. The word, like the δαίμων, confronts man not as a creation of his own, but as an objective reality existing in its own right. Indeed, Usener's work begins with a forthright statement to the effect:

It is not by any voluntary act that the name of a thing is established. People do not invent a pleasing complex of sounds in order to introduce it, like a coin, as the sign of a particular thing. The spiritual excitement evoked by some encountered

[11] Usener, *Götternamen: Versuch einer Lehre von der religiösen Begriffsbildung,* 3te Auflag (Frankfurt/M.: G. Schulte-Bulmke, 1948), pp. 280, 290–91.

117

object in the outer world is simultaneously the occasion and the medium of its appellation. Sensory impressions are what the self receives in its meeting with the not-self, and the liveliest of these strive naturally towards vocal expression: they are the bases of separate appellations which the speaking populace attempts.[12]

Corresponding with the birth of the "momentary gods," then, is the genesis of language, whose primary function was likewise not to compare things or to select their common properties, but to intensify experience and to be its distilled essence. Myth still concentrates upon the uniqueness of the event and its immediate appearance, while language, arising out of a similar kind of apprehension, has developed discursive habits. Yet both are children of the same parents, according to Usener: they both spring from spiritual excitement and inner tension by the same mental process.

The fact that words have acquired an existence which is independent of their origin means that we entertain two attitudes towards the use of language, each of which stands in its own relation to its origin. Mythical thinking and religious language reflect their direct participation in the reality they describe; discursive thinking and theoretical language express their freedom through adaptability to every phase of life.

In the Hebrew Scriptures "the word of the Lord" initiates the very events it forthtells; the name of the Lord is not only a "strong tower," but is identical with God. This closeness of word to reality appears also in the Christian Scriptures. Jesus is recorded as saying: "Where two or three are gathered together in *my name,* there am *I* . . ." (Matt. 18:20, AV); and the prologue of the Fourth Gospel, which

[12] *Ibid.,* p. 3.

speaks of the word as God's agent in creation, also says, "what the Word was, God was" (John 1:1, NEB).

But loosed from this original unity in which word and event were one and the same, theoretical thinking has become functional and uses words as tools or instruments for expressing relationships and for forming systematic connections between events and things within the totality of life. This disconnectedness from their origins, and consequent remoteness from any one specific datum, has given to words a freedom of movement which enables them to connect phenomena with each other. They stand in a mediating position and are symbols of relationships.

We may deplore the loss to our society of what Laurens van der Post has called the "whole natural language of the spirit," yet the contrast between discursive and mythical thinking is by no means so well defined or so absolute as some people fear or the orderly mind may wish, for we are obliged to confess that science itself uses poetic language and depends upon myth-making. We marvel at the scents of flowers, reflections in water, and "the night's starr'd face"; then this world of sense experience is described, interpreted and classified for us, and because we desire knowledge we accept the propositions set before us as being true. Like apparatus, the mechanism of things is dismantled; the anatomy and physiology of nature is laid bare. But subsequently we learn that the entire spectrum of phenomena can be reduced to the atom, and that the atom itself may be understood as a microcosmic, planetary system of electrons whirling around their solar nuclei, neutron and proton. Of this infinitesimal cosmos none has direct sensory experience; the explanation is an image, and the physicist has been pressed into a poetic mode of thinking; his knowledge is clothed in metaphor, and his probing is attested by a work of art.

If these "fiducial elements" contained in science reflect its origins, then the characteristics of its thinking processes —its sense of order, its habit of exact thought, and its belief that every occurrence can be correlated with antecedents and seen to exemplify a general principle—reflect the formative power of historical Christianity upon it, especially habits of Scholastic reasoning and insistence upon the rationality of God. Indeed, faith in the possibility of science is "an unconscious derivative of medieval theology." [13]

Human thinking has journeyed far since men believed in the magical power of words and used them to "control" their environment, but today we must ask of language: Have words strayed too far from man's life? We recognise that they diminish in power when uprooted from their native soil:

> Words strain,
> Crack and sometimes break, under the burden,
> Under the tension, slip, slide, perish,
> Decay with imprecision, will not stay in place,
> Will not stay still.[14]

[13] Alfred North Whitehead, *Science and the Modern World* (New York: Macmillan, 1925), p. 18. Cf. Pierre Teilhard de Chardin, *The Phenomenon of Man* (London: Collins, 1959), p. 284: "Neither in its impetus nor in its achievements can science go to its limits without becoming tinged with mysticism and charged with faith."

In the present time there are forces external both to science and to religion which may press from them a confession of relatedness. Albert Camus informed us that modern unbelief was no longer based upon science—as it had been at the end of the last century. "It denies the faith of science as much as that of religion. It is no longer the scepticism of reason in face of miracles but rather a passionate unbelief" (*une incroyance passionnée*). *Les Cahiers du Sud* (April 1943), pp. 306–11.

[14] T. S. Eliot, "Burnt Norton, V," *Four Quartets* (New York: Harcourt, Brace & World, Inc.); also in *Collected Poems, 1909–1935* (London: Faber and Faber, 1936), p. 190.

But we regard this also as a mark of their growth: new attachments loosen old associations, and fresh conceptions of life emerge. Yet the question remains: Are words too "objectified"? In the service of life's many interests, have words become estranged from life as a whole? In granting to language a freedom of association, has man bestowed upon it a degree of independence of his well-being sufficient to endanger him? Has dissociation from their sources endowed words with powers inimical to life? Are there too many free-floating theses which deprive man of a basic sense of proportion in face of the physical world?

Unqualified replies are not suited to these questions, yet immediately we speak of language as occupying a mediating position between man and the world, or of words as symbols of man's relationship with it, we recall that underlying all speech and language are conceptual models and ways of encountering the world.

When language was close to "revelation," alive in its own glory and delight, the presence of a thing could be evoked by the use of its name. But usage reduces this evocative power, and names become literary words from which both the excitement of being and the quality of intensity have withdrawn. Religious people often hold firmly and instinctively to particular words and concepts lest, divorced from specific events, their language lose its characteristics. They fear that once the characteristics of language change, experiences themselves may vanish and life itself be threatened with disruption. Nevertheless, religious language, unexempt from the attritions of time and custom, is demythologised in the interests of intelligibility. But even the acknowledgement that "man doth not live by bread only" may not permit us to assume that with the dietary addition of a *rational* word we shall be adequately nourished and preserved whole. The mystery of existence is not annulled by baptism into the name of a soluble problem; the rite could mean initiation into a life divorced from the depths of its own being.

Rational language is assumed to constitute authentic communication between persons, but may not convey all the qualities and attitudes which belong to human existence; its authenticity will depend upon conceptual models of the world and human being, and upon the mythopoeic which nourishes rationality. Language itself cannot plumb the depths of existence by descent from its surface, as though there were given truths whose existence matched the formulae with which we sought them. It would therefore be unreal and improper to isolate language and attach blame to it for "irresponsibility"; its limitations and its sufficiency reflect man's vision of the world and of himself, so that our conceptual models, hardened by usage in the charged and changing atmosphere of time endured, need to be re-fashioned in a fresh access of light. Indeed, after having given ourselves away to things, survival may now depend upon a new light in which we discover all things *in ourselves*. Such an awareness, measured conceptually in psycho-somatic, environmental and personal categories, would require the force of revelation; that is to say, its linguistic and conceptual frameworks would have to authenticate themselves to multitudes by sound, by feeling and by concrete images of a personal unity of man and things.

In pursuit of this suggestion concerning the estrangement of language from man's total life, or from genuine interest in his survival, it is perhaps worth noticing that certain writers of novels allow things to "preponderate" over human beings. Virginia Woolf sometimes made remarkably little distinction between things and people. In Germany, Gerd Gaiser, who is considered to be an important "mainstream" novelist, has written the life story of a mountain (*Das Schiff im Berg*). This turning from man to nature has been regarded by some criticis as "antihumanism," but set alongside the scientific inquiry which appraises natural phenomena in human terms—the lost "memory" of proliferating cells in the human body; the selective ability of the "crystal membrane"—is this literary genre not equally worth considering as a humanisation of the world? If, in place of the daemons of mediaeval times, the scientific spirit has surrounded our lives with blind, inexorable forces, so that we are hemmed in by a determinism from which it is extremely difficult, if not impossible, to break loose, may we not regard the "humanising" of the world as a countermeasure to this threat, and the expression of a desire to protect those personal qualities so easily lost in the commerce of life and the traffic of words?

One of the appendices in William Temple's work *Nature, Man and God* concludes with this expression of the "kinship" of mind and reality:

When I say that Mind finds itself or what is akin to itself in its object, I mean an experience which has two aspects: first, that it finds the counterpart of the principles of its own activities as for example the mathematical properties of mechanical combinations of forces or of aesthetic proportions; secondly, that with this discovery goes a feeling of being at home with the object, not lost or bewildered in presence of it. The latter aspect is not capable of definition, but seems to me to be easily recognizable and profoundly significant.[15]

If, therefore, our appraisals of the world are an aspect of

[15] Appendix to the chapter entitled "Truth and Beauty" (London: Macmillan, 1953), p. 165.

ourselves, language and concept will more specifically and consciously relate themselves to our survival, and to man's continuing life in this world. A personal or "humane" nomenclature will reject the alternatives of spirit and matter in order to participate in the inwardness and outwardness of things; the empathy (*Einfühlung*) of language, uniting with matter, will initiate the return of nature from its estrangement into the household of man.

The reference to empathy should not force us to abandon the suggestion as "emotional"; for "only poetic empathy opens the inner life of nature" (Tillich). The term describes the attitude of the human being who chooses himself: intelligence, imagination, the will to survive; and in this choice he seeks to overcome his estrangement from nature and to be at home in this world. A brash, pulsating thought from Unamuno shall herald our later discussion of the character of empathy. He says that although the action of reason be to mechanise or materialise the world, the work of man is to "supernaturalize" it. This, he explains, is to make it divine by making it human, to help it to become conscious of itself,[16] for consciousness is participated knowledge; it is co-feeling, com-passion. And on the premise that "love personalizes all that it loves," Unamuno ventures to say that only by personalising everything could we possibly love everything, but that such world-embracing love—"the instinct of perpetuation"—would disclose to us that "the Universe is also a Person possessing a Consciousness. . . . And this Consciousness of the Universe, which love, personalizing all that it loves, discovers, is what we call God." [17]

[16] Unamuno, *The Tragic Sense of Life* (New York: Dover, 1954), p. 151.

[17] *Ibid.*, p. 139.

Will the earth not require man's care and compassion if, together with its inhabitants, it is to pursue its creative way? Is it not necessary for men in all disciplines to develop a language which expresses responsibility for themselves within their physical environment? Do we not need a language of care to symbolise and encourage the growth of commensurate behaviour? Is not our choice of language a matter of life or death? If it is, and man is destined to share yet more profoundly in the life of the cosmos, while the world participates more richly in his life, then he may be obliged to choose both faith and language akin to the Unamunian credo, which states: "I believe that the Universe possesses a certain consciousness like myself, because its action towards me is a human action, and I feel that it is a personality that environs me." [18]

[18] *Ibid.*, p. 195.

7

A Personal Universe

The work of charity, of the love of God, is to endeavour to liberate God from brute matter, to endeavour to give consciousness to everything; it is to dream that the very rocks may find a voice and work in accordance with the spirit of this dream; it is to dream that everything that exists may become conscious, that the Word may become life.

Miguel de Unamuno [1]

The only universe capable of containing the human person is an irreversibly 'personalising' universe.

Pierre Teilhard de Chardin [2]

BECAUSE WE ARE human beings our knowledge of the world is always anthropomorphic in character. When we distinguish between human beings and material things, the characteristics we attribute to things are a selection from those we ascribe to persons. If religion is accused of anthropomorphism, then by virtue of the models it constructs, science cannot avoid being similarly implicated. The characteristics of material objects are also those of human beings. John Macmurray brings this home to us by saying that unless we had fallen downstairs, or otherwise lost control of our physical movements, we could not understand what was meant by "a body falling freely through space," and he states this particular aspect of our knowing in a general way by saying:

[1] *The Tragic Sense of Life* (New York: Dover, 1954), p. 214.
[2] *The Phenomenon of Man* (London: Collins, 1959), p. 290.

The concept of 'a person' is inclusive of the concept of 'an organism', as the concept of 'an organism' is inclusive of that of 'a material body'. The included concepts can be derived from the concept of 'a person' by abstractions; by excluding from attention those characters which belong to the higher category alone.[3]

This process of abstraction or exclusion, Macmurray explains, is the genesis of our dualism of "mind" and "matter." Having abstracted the concept of a "material" object from the concept of a "person," we illegitimately form a concept of mind on the basis of what we excluded from that of a "person" in order to state the concept of a "thing," as though this were an independently existing entity. In this way the idea of the "nonmaterial," or "mind" or "consciousness" as existing in themselves was born. And he suggests that this dualistic interpretation of reality, which has been of immense usefulness hitherto, now approaches a point of exhaustion where it should be met and superseded by another category of understanding, better able to penetrate the nature of the world with vitality and hope for the future of man.

The tensions of our time and the dissimilarities of social structure, so emotionally accentuated in political debate, point to what must be the *essential* question at this moment of the world's history. It is the problem of *remaining human* within any of the systems under which mankind is now organized. Our tendency to deify the State or to seek our *raison d'être* in external configurations of authority reflect the difficulty we have in assuming personal responsibility. This reluctance to be answerable for ourselves is rooted in our exposure to freedom, and our nakedness before the

[3] *The Self as Agent* (London: Faber and Faber, 1957), p. 117.

future. Freedom hides within itself the necessity of making decisions which prescribe our future, whose shape, nevertheless, we cannot accurately delineate. Freedom forces us to say who we are, and therefore to act in the light of whom we hope to become. But because we can have no practical certainty of the outcome of our decisions, and are haunted by a desire for security, our difficulty is one of acting in good faith, and of believing in our future as persons, regardless of the indeterminable outcome of our choices. In this vertigo of freedom we hold on to life in such a way as to endanger our future, and the apotheosis of political authority accentuates the fact that, in face of the hazards of existence and the terrors of freedom, men are prepared to "function" rather than to "live," and will sacrifice personal values to broader and less discriminating expediencies. But this brief description of what has been called "the crisis of the personal" may be differently stated when visualised within the context of philosophy and science.

Behind our dangers to personal existence lie categories of thought; concepts created by philosophy and used by science to unlock the mystery of the world. Descartes's predominant categories of extended and thinking *substance* were translated into scientific endeavour which made important advances towards understanding and determining the physical world, but could not wholly unlock the mystery of what human reality is, for in order to evaluate the world in terms of substance a constructive spontaneity of mind is required which seems to be without *substantial* basis. In view of man's inwardness, his determining and directing capacities, it becomes impossible to understand man within the form of the material; so that, confronted by the spontaneity which attends processes of growth, the concept of the material yielded to that of the organism. The organic was conceived of as an harmonious balancing of differences, and in the context of life and becoming was represented as "a dynamic equilibrium of functions maintained through a progressive differentiation of elements within the whole." [4] Man is not substance but organism; thought is no longer mathematical but dialectical, not analytic but synthetic; it progresses through a synthesis of opposites. This concept of the organic encouraged the development of the biological sciences, but in its turn reached the breaking point in confrontation with human beings, for so long as we understand ourselves in terms of the organic our social planning, for example, will push us towards a totalitarian society.

This category of the organic and its consequence for human beings had been strongly challenged by Søren Kierkegaard in his dispute with Idealism. He regarded the organic as a limiting concept inadequate for compassing the facts of our existence, whose contingencies are not determinable by us. The organic meant thinking of reality as a finite whole, and he asked how such complete knowledge could be claimed, or by what authority man—a "synthesis of the infinite and the finite . . . of freedom and necessity" [5]—can be reduced to a system or an organism. He understood that the category of the organic had been designed as a protest on behalf of life against an interpretation of reality in mechanistic terms, but believed that in the course of its development or application, it had become a more sophisticated and, therefore, a more dangerous form of determinism, undermining the genuineness of the concept of freedom.

Subsequently, our human collectivities have been seen to

[4] *Ibid.*, p. 33.

[5] *The Sickness unto Death* (Princeton: Princeton University Press, 1941), p. 17.

rest upon an organised atrophy of personal existence; we are realising that the organisation of men and techniques must be more healthily informed than for the production of wealth and power, and will derive a more genuinely authoritative existence when inspired by the advent of a world of persons.

Our technological accomplishments—so perfectly objective and altogether explicable, so impressive, so menacing and depersonalising in their power—have succeeded in bending some of their creators to a belief in man's helplessness vis-à-vis his creations, as though his destiny were one of utter subjection to the forces of the earth. This danger calls for a new category of understanding in which man's scientific and technological prowess may "personalise" the universe rather than depersonalise man himself, and our collectivities move in the direction of communities in which interpersonal existence is increased and confirmed. But in this abstract existence of inhumanity and mechanical power a new category of understanding is emerging in which man is regarded as *person,* and the world, therefore, as "personal."

Man's exploitation of nature is not destined to erect upon the web of natural determinism another net-work of conditioned reflexes; it is to open up before the creative liberty of an ever-increasing number of men, the highest possibilities of human being.[6]

Emmanuel Mounier's new and courageous evaluation of the meaning of our technological society demands that we become aware of the universe, not as an abstraction but as a presence; that we regard man, not as a conscious actor

[6] Emmanuel Mounier, *Personalism* (London: Routledge & Kegan Paul, 1952), p. 12.

before an unconscious backdrop, but as a knowing subject who perceives himself as the object of knowledge, and knows that he is the key to the science of nature, the solution of everything we can know; and that to decipher man in his totality is to try to find out how the world was made, and how it ought to go on making itself.

At many points in recorded history "personalising" tendencies are recognisable. The famous inscription at Delphi —KNOW THYSELF—challenged man's subservience to blind destiny and his absorption in tribe and city. The advent of Christianity sharpened the notion of individual responsibility, and Christianity has sought to be the exponent and guardian of the personal. If men have not actively engaged, like Martin Luther, in the adventure of responsible liberty, then at least like Walt Whitman, they have surveyed their "democratic vistas" and have beheld man "divine in his own right" and "untouchable by any canons of authority." With Whitman they have believed that beneath the fluctuations of society and the movements of politics—"the immense tendencies towards aggregation"—they discern processes which are clarifying the image of the complete man, strengthening his individual, personal dignity.[7]

The "personalist" movement in France, whose voices echoed through the pages of *Esprit* from 1932 onwards, attempted both to combat the mounting political and spiritual crisis in Europe and to assert within it the existence of man as a creative person. At the heart of its constructions lay a principle of unpredictability and a recognition of the uniqueness of each individual which forbade those processes of abstraction that treat of human beings as types. In

[7] *Democratic Vistas and Other Papers* (London: Walter Scott, 1888), pp. 17–18.

defining the essence of the person, Emmanuel Mounier says that our reality as human beings is not exhausted by all the ways in which we express ourselves and impinge upon the world, nor is it entirely subjected to anything by which we are conditioned. It is neither an internal substratum beneath our attitudes nor an abstract principle of overt behaviour, but the living activity of self-creation, communication and attachment that "grasps and knows itself, in the act, as the *movement of becoming personal.*" [8]

The personalists argued and Mounier in particular, that human beings are not even the most marvellous objects in a world of objects, "like mobile trees or a more astute kind of animal"; the person is "the one reality that we know, and that we are at the same time fashioning, from within. Present everywhere, it is *given* nowhere." [9] We are not objects separable from the world but centres of its reorientation, not souls in bodies but "wholly body and wholly spirit."

In emphasising the inseparable earthiness and spirituality of man, contributors to *Esprit* recognised that they enunciated nothing new, but were stressing what they believed their generation required. For Thomas Aquinas had asserted the existential unity of body and soul, and what the personalists say is often reminiscent of the passionate philosophy of Miguel de Unamuno, for whom there are no things in themselves and no metaphysically absolute nature beneath sensible experience. Unamuno expresses no basic propositions about the nature of reality, and although he uses the language of inwardness, this does not designate "hidden" realities; for his noumena are not opposed to

[8] Mounier, *Personalism*, p. x.
[9] *Ibid.*, p. x.

phenomena, nor does reality stand over against appearances. The real does not constitute the foundation of appearances, nor does it consist in phenomena themselves, but rather of the inwardness and outwardness of things. The true reality is neither matter nor spirit, neither flesh nor soul; "matter as such" and "spirit as such" are not real, they are mere abstractions which lack what has been called "incessantly palpitating intimacy."

So personalism, avoiding the extremes of materialism and spiritism, states that man is a body in the same degree that he is a spirit, that the real is intrareal, that it is of the essence of matter to bear a spiritual character and of spirit to participate in matter.

Upon this understanding of the nature of the world the personalists sought to live the experiment of a personal life exposing themselves as beings rather than functions, trusting to evoke a personal response to their self-disclosure, and also to express the purpose of the world, summed up for them in the emergence of creative personality. Though personalisation, strictly speaking, began only with man, they believed it possible to discern a preparation for man's personal existence throughout the history of the universe. Observing in descriptions of the physical world that the concept of determinism was yielding to one of choice or liberty, and that in the infinitesimal world of the atom, for example, no more than a "pseudo-causality" [10] was apparent, they were encouraged to pursue the possibility of studying the external world in order to show that the personal mode of existing is the highest form of existence,

[10] The same cause may produce one or another of several possible effects with only a certain probability that such and such an effect will be produced and not another.

and that the evolution of prehuman nature converges upon a creative moment, or crosses a threshold of reflection, beyond which man is able to say to himself that thus far the universe has evolved, that to this reflectiveness or to this altruism the world has attained. Its central reality seems to be an act of personalisation, and the impersonal realities, so called, the material earth with its flora and fauna, are part of this process of the world towards personalisation.

The most persuasive presentation of the category of the personal for the understanding of the natural world is contained in the posthumously published work of Pierre Teilhard de Chardin, *The Phenomenon of Man,* which is an account of the nature and destiny of the world. He argues that inasmuch as man is its key figure, mindlike properties must be present in all its material systems throughout the universe. Matter, "this primordial dust of consciousness," has within itself an innate tendency towards the production of more complex structures, so that from simple inorganic material more complex bodies appear. Under suitable conditions, these in turn become living organisms, moving from simplicity to complexity, cradling the anthropoids and culminating in man. But even in man the same creative urge or tendency obtains, and here Teilhard is reminiscent of Nietzsche's Zarathustra, for whom "man is a bridge." Teilhard's man is as yet unfinished and to be surpassed; he is preparing a more complex society in which his social tendencies will be complemented by the achievement of a truly personal existence, expressing the deepest essence of a growing universe.

Teilhard's stupendous vision, described with colourful vitality, has not made its appearance in unrelated fashion or without recognisable ancestry, for Karl Marx and Rainer

Maria Rilke were heralds of its advent. The truth of Teilhard's vision is embodied mythologically in Rilke's *Stories of God*. His account "Of One Who Listened to the Stones" [11] describes how Michelangelo's hands hovered listening about the uncut stone, and how that attentiveness to its possibilities evoked questions of why a man should listen to stones, and whether or not they have souls! When the sculptor's hands awoke and tore at the stones "as at a grave, from which flickers a faint, dying voice," God asked him, "Michelangelo, who is in that stone?" he replied, "Thou, my God, who else? But I cannot reach Thee." And God sensed that he was in the stone, "fearful and confined," hoping for the hands of Michelangelo to deliver him, "and he heard them coming, though as yet afar." Then with broad strokes Michelangelo set free the figures of a Pieta. But when mysteriously drawn and incarcerated within the narrow confines of his room whose walls leaned upon him so that he let himself be shaped by them, there came a voice, "Michelangelo, who is in thee?" And he replied, "Thou, my God, who else?" whereupon "all became wide around God, and he freely lifted up his face . . . and there was no end to the heavens."

Rilke, too, endeavours to fathom the meaning of things and to penetrate to their utmost core in order to grasp, and if possible to spell out, their ultimate significance. He communes with God, whom he senses not only in the persons of the poor and the outcast, but also in animals, inanimate objects and natural phenomena. His search for the significance of things is simultaneously a search for the presence and reality of God who, because he is the ubiqui-

[11]Rilke, *Stories of God,* trans. by M. D. Herter Norton and Nora Purtscher-Wydenbruch (New York: Norton, 1932), pp. 115–21.

tous inwardness of things, can reveal himself in anything. And in this search man is the key to the release and increase of God.

Teilhard draws our attention not only to the mechanical and mathematical movement of matter but also to the evolution of life and consciousness within its ever increasing complexity as it involutes upon itself, and it is difficult to dismiss the thought that his view was also foreshadowed by Marx and Engels.

Like Marx, Teilhard seeks to avoid the use of the word "spirit," and speaks of the "two energies" and of the dynamic relationships existing between the "within" and the "without" of things: and he is forced to conclude that "in last analysis, *somehow or other,* there must be a single energy operating in the world." [12] This is reminiscent of Marx, for whom "abstract materialism" and "abstract spiritualism" come to the same thing; it is not a matter of choosing the one or the other, but of accepting "the truth that unites them both" beyond their separation.

In Teilhard's view it is not merely life and movement which inhere in matter, but also consciousness and purpose.

. . . on the plane of animate particles, we find the fundamental technique of *groping,* . . . This groping strangely combines the blind fantasy of large numbers with the precise orientation of a specific target. It would be a mistake to see it as mere chance. Groping is *directed chance.*[13]

Thus the energy which is immanent in the evolutionary process itself guides it by a natural way of trial and error to ever more "improbable" constructions.

In this brief comparison of Teilhard's vision with that of

[12] *The Phenomenon of Man,* p. 63.
[13] *Ibid.,* p. 110.

Marx their understanding of the place and future of man is worth noting also. Comparable with Teilhard's view of the world is the position which Marx accords to man. He affirms that "the criticism of religion ends with the teaching that man is the highest essence for man, hence with the categoric imperative to overthrow all relations in which man is a debased, enslaved, abandoned, despicable essence." [14] With regard to the future of man, Marx begins with the view that "the primary forms of matter are the living, individualizing *forces of being* inherent in it," [15] and from this conviction of the inseparability of the material and the personal he has to say "how necessarily materialism is connected with communism and socialism.[16] If man is shaped by his surroundings, his surroundings must be made human, and if man is social by nature, "he will develop his true nature only in society, and the power of his nature must be measured not by the power of separate individuals but by the power of society." [17]

According to Teilhard man's evolutionary pathway also lies in the direction of a socialisation of man. The entire human phylum must converge upon itself after the manner of the evolutionary drive in all things. This convergence of a world which furls its elements upon themselves must precipitate persons upon one another, but only when we mistake individuality for personality do we assume that their number and proximity forebodes a return to the impersonal. "In trying to separate itself as much as possible from others, the element individualises itself; but in doing

[14] *On Religion* (Moscow: Foreign Languages Publishing House, 1956), p. 50.

[15] *The Holy Family* (Moscow: Foreign Languages Publishing House, 1956), p. 172.

[16] *Ibid.*, p. 176.

[17] *Ibid.*, p. 176.

so it becomes retrograde and seeks to drag the world backwards towards plurality and into matter. . . . To be fully ourselves it is in the opposite direction, in the direction of convergence with all the rest, that we must advance— towards the 'other.' " [18] In conformity with the evolutionary structure of the world we can discover our persons only by uniting together; the convergence of humanity upon itself is the condition of man's greater personalisation.

And in the establishment now proceeding through science and the philosophies of a collective human *Weltanschauung* in which every one of us co-operates and participates, are we not experiencing the first symptoms of an aggregation of a still higher order, the birth of some single centre from the convergent beams of millions of elementary centres dispersed over the surface of the thinking earth? [19]

In Teilhard's view, union *differentiates:* and in this collective, the "Omega point," which concentrates and assembles all consciousnesses and all the conscious, each element acquires more distinctness in proportion to its proximity to the centre. It is a socialism which personalises.

At this point Teilhard surpasses our experience, and contradicts the distressing aspects of modern attempts at collectivisation. Hitherto, man has gone about the business of his unification with mediocre, utilitarian purposes in mind, resulting in the enslavement rather than a liberation of "consciousness." Teilhard is deeply aware of this, yet dares to affirm that "love alone is capable of uniting living beings in such a way as to complete and fulfil them" [20] and that it

[18] *The Phenomenon of Man,* p. 263.
[19] *Ibid.,* p. 259.
[20] *Ibid.,* p. 265.

alone is the energy which unites men without destroying them. However, the word "love" does not here refer to the sentimental face of love, but to its full biological reality. The affinity of being with being is a general property of all life, and this propensity of things to unite at a "prodigiously rudimentary level" makes it possible for love to appear in "hominised" form. Indeed, to be certain of the presence of love in ourselves we must assume its presence in an inchoate form in everything that is.[21]

Against the argument that love as we understand it is highly selective and exclusive, Teilhard sets the instinct which moves us towards unity, our sense of the *universe,* our "resonance to the All." Our description of love in terms of human relationships extending, perhaps, to love of country, does not exhaust love's natural forms. Indeed, it omits their very *raison d'être,* namely, the cosmic affinity evinced by the stuff of the world as it converges upon itself and integrates, both locally and universally, to become interpersonal reality. Thus, loving the universe is the only complete and final way in which we can love. A universe in terms of immensity and number into which the person is absorbed conjures up an essentially unlovable collectivity, whereas a universe which personalises itself—not by becoming a person, but by developing a focus of personal energies and attractions—will encourage the love that is everywhere trying to be born.

[21] Teilhard is consciously drawing upon Nicholas of Cusa, for whom each finite thing mirrors the whole universe, but none so clearly as man who combines in himself matter, organic life, sensitive animal life and spiritual rationality. Man is the world in miniature, embracing within himself the intellectual and material aspects of reality. (*De docta ignorantia: Of Learned Ignorance,* trans. G. Heron [New Haven: Yale University Press, 1954], Book 3, Chap. III, pp. 134–37.)

8

Accepting the World

No business serious seemed but one, no work
But one was found; and that did in me lurk.
  D'ye ask me what? It was with clearer eyes
To see all creatures full of Deities;
Especially one's self: And to admire
The satisfaction of all true desire:
'Twas to be pleased with all that God hath done;
'Twas to enjoy even all beneath the sun:
'Twas with a steady and immediate sense
To feel and measure all the excellence
Of things; 'twas to inherit endless treasure,
And to be filled with everlasting pleasure:

Thomas Traherne [1]

With openness I surrendered my heart to the grave and suffering
earth, and frequently in pensive hour, promised to love it faith-
fully unto death, without fear, with all its fatality and mystery.
Thus solemnly did I bind myself to it for ever.

Friedrich Hölderlin [2]

THE MORE THE NINETEENTH CENTURY recedes the less comprehensible becomes its opposition of science to religion. The more the twentieth century unfolds the less dogmatic become the men of science and of faith, and the more do their beliefs and systems partake of a "principle of uncertainty."

[1] From "Dumbness," *The Poetical Works of Thomas Traherne* (London: Bertram Dobell, 1906), pp. 34–37.

[2] From *"Der Tod des Empedokles"* (Weimar: Utopia Verlag, 1923),

Under some political systems scientific exploration is geared to a "materialistic" view of life, and research is bound by dogmatism; under others in which scientists are not professionally obliged to cultivate a particular political awareness, science is still defined as "essentially a means of obtaining practical mastery over nature." When we consider that "nature" includes human nature, it is not difficult to imagine scientific processes anywhere in the world, leading to the subordination of man to science, and of science to theories and teachings which generate forms of unwisdom from which disastrous consequences could flow.

This modern attitude to the universe and human life is sharply contrasted with the θεωρία or contemplation of the ancients. When reality was conceived of as something given and unchangeable, man's problem was to subdue his life to its dictates and to be conformed to the conditions it imposed. Hölderlin's Empedocles expresses his desire to conform to the nature of the earth: "ihr mein Leben so *zu eignen* bis zuletzt." In modern times the problem is how to subdue reality to man's desires, and how to make it conformable to his aspirations. From the pursuit of wisdom in order to control himself man has sought to acquire knowledge in order to control his environment.

We shall probably agree that it is not enough for human

Gesammelte Werke, IV, p. 113. In the quotation I give roughly the sense of the following lines:

> *"Die Beste Seele gern*
> *Den Sterblichen und furchtlos offen gab*
> *Mein Herz wie du der ernsten Erde sich,*
> *Der schicksalvollen; ach! ihr treu zu bleiben*
> *Gelobt ich, und ein Jüngling, ihr*
> *Mein Leben so zu eignen bis zuletzt.*
> *Ich sagt ihr's oft in trauter Stunde zu,*
> *Band so den teuern Todesbund mit ihr."*

beings to conform to the natural world out of which they proceed, or merely to react against nature's provocations.

In most realms of investigation "pure curiosity" is suspect; our knowledge is related to our needs; "nothing is known which has not been previously wanted" (Unamuno); so that the will rather than intelligence bears an initial responsibility for our understanding of the world.

The scientific frame of mind entertains a distinct attitude to nature. The idea that scientists humbly attend upon facts is false if it implies that scientific processes are passively followed. Scientists ask definite questions of nature, and the answers with which nature presents them are already hidden in their enquiries. The nature of the question determines the ensuing kind of science. Francis Bacon called this technique "putting nature to the question"—a phrase which savours of the Inquisition. Yet this is the *experimental* method of our time, enfolding a degree of compulsiveness unsought by empirical enquiry.

But if the compulsiveness in man's relation to nature is like that existing between master and slave, then the situation bears no augury of ultimate freedom. Persons achieve freedom in conferring it. Our liberation is bound up with the liberation of things. Marx stated that the reduction of things to commodities degraded them, and that to be made merely instrumental to profit deprived them of their intrinsic dignity. We ourselves will contribute to this degradation whenever we use things as obstacles to be overcome or as stuff to be possessed. This power exercised over things has a habit of communicating itself to human relations and infusing them with a tyrannical spirit.

It is therefore not enough to say, as we have done, that the relation between man and things is one in which nature acquires a human meaning as men define its essences, or

142

that nature thus defined becomes a reflection of man's reality. The prior question is, Who is man? How shall he be defined in order that he may define nature? Must we not define him as *person*? And then, although we deny nature as it is given in order to affirm it as a task, the task becomes both personal and the condition of all personality. Our task will still be to transform nature, but to transform it into the image of a personal universe.

How shall we move towards this personal concept of the world? A recognition of what is real and actual seems to be an important first step in this direction. We may accept with reservations our immediate, natural environment, but our finest regard for it will be determined by our acceptance of the world in its entirety. But is this total acceptance possible, particularly in view of the cruelty, the ugliness and the evil which we discern in its structures?

Man shares many qualities with other living things, and the evolutionary process by which their great diversity has been brought about has moulded our human stock as well. All organisms have a unity in which we share: our physical being possesses the basic regulatory character which all living material displays by unfolding itself in conformity with an immanent pattern so as to reach a condition of wholeness. There is much evidence among the higher animals pointing to the beginnings of those rational, emotional and moral traits which we regard as man's highest qualities, so that the origins of his physical life do not need to involve the interjection into him of anything radically new or different.[3] There is a sense, therefore, in which the sociology of nature points to man's being-at-home in the world.

[3] This thesis is persuasively expounded by Edmund W. Sinnott in *The Biology of the Spirit* (London: Gollancz, 1956) and also summarised in an essay in the symposium entitled, *What Is the Nature of Man?* (Philadelphia: Christian Education Press, 1959).

Despite its "inhuman" or "impersonal" treatment of individuals or communities the universe has become the enveloping tissue of man's life; it has nurtured him; it is his *Heimat*. Our grievances against the universe are born of its assaults upon our private happiness or security, but even in face of the precariousness of our existence it is impossible to maintain that the universe is inimical to mankind as a whole. Has not the solar system been the nursery within which man was born and has grown up? Is it not now his home as he reaches his majority?

On all hands the power of evil has been seriously recognised in our time. Jean-Paul Sartre has gone so far as to attribute to it an absoluteness like that of good. But in accordance with the understanding of reality and the nature of knowledge which we have described, good cannot exist in solitary splendour, nor is it opposed by a radically separate evil with which it has nothing to do. Light is not the opposite of shade; nor is shade the absence of light. They appear simultaneously, the one emphasising the presence of the other. Similarly evil is bound up with good in such a way that both are parts of a whole, and we must recognise the reality of evil without affirming its permanence. It is never completely divorced from good; and is capable of being transformed, for example, by man's use of its energies in the service of good. Martin Buber has been quoted as saying: "One must love evil . . . even as evil wishes to be loved." [4] For the world is not a being over against us. It is a becoming. We do not have to accept it as it is, for we are continually creating it, not only by bestowing upon our

[4] Cf. Martin Buber's article, *"Ueber Jakob Boehme," Wiener Rundschau*, Vol. V, No. 12 (15th June, 1901), pp. 251–53.

perceptions a firmness which makes them into a reality, but also by letting our strength flow into the becoming, so that we ourselves enter into the world of destiny and become shaping elements in the great event. Man's arm is a river, and the fingers of his hand a delta. Down the river flows a stream of energy, rising in far-off sources of the mind and spirit; and through the delta of the fingers the stream of energy empties upon the ocean of events, contributing to the visible and invisible life of the world.

Man's biological unity with the world might be a basis for regarding all things positively, but the fact that he is capable of doing to the earth, and so to himself, what he ought not to do, demands that he seek a renewed spring of love enabling him to endure the whole reality of lived life, to transcend nature by creating rather than by destroying, and to pursue the disciplines of a "science of survival."

This freedom to create and to change the world cannot be said to subvert its regularity or to stultify its science; but to suspend painful and tragic events as evil would be to substitute for physical order a chaos of incalculable miracle. Physical evil must necessarily be. That we are obliged to live with it, if we are to live at all, and that man has made his evolutionary pilgrimage within such an environment is evident; yet the question remains, *How* are we to live with it? In estrangement and hostility, coexistently or in community? Shall we accept a part of it, and condemn a part? Or must we learn to accept the whole?

Man's future seems to lie with the acceptance of the whole, but the idea of the acceptance of the world in its totality needs to be defined, for we can say we accept the whole without accepting the whole of ourselves, and total acceptance of the world requires this existential self-inclusion for its validity.

There is an attitude of passive acceptance vividly portrayed in the work of Bertolt Brecht whose early poetry (*Hauspostille*) and drama (*Baal*) reflect those surfaces of horror and atrocity which characterised the German baroque theatre. His pervading themes are death and decomposition in all its forms: the entire flora and fauna of decay. But the passionate lamentation of human misery in baroque drama becomes in Brecht a representation of the metamorphoses of nature, or the processes of life, containing a certain spiritual depth and joy. His "Great Thanksgiving Chorale" speaks in the following fashion:

Praise the tree which thrives upon carrion, exulting heaven-high,
Praise the carrion,
Praise the tree that devoured it,
But praise also the sky.[5]

Brecht expresses a docile love of all things, a serene acquiescence in the natural world, a sense of brotherhood with plants and animals and all transitory life, as though one should live this span of life indifferently, without rancour or anxiety, "lazy and in the end content," with a this-worldly piety expressing itself in the acceptance of the natural order without exception. His poem "Of the Friendliness of the World" describes the arrival of the child, at the mercy of any who might care, helpless upon the indifferent,

[5] "*Gesammtausgabe*," *Gedichte* I, 1918–29 (Frankfurt a/M: Suhrkamp Verlag, 1960), p. 74. The English is a translation of the following verse:
"*Lobet den Baum, der aus Aas aufwächst jauchzend zum Himmel!*
Lobet das Aas
Lobet den Baum, der es frass
Aber auch lobet den Himmel."

windswept earth, and the departure of the adult, scarred and decrepit, who nevertheless, almost certainly has *loved* the world.[6]

This docility which awakens our imagination, were it effected, might give comfort to some individuals, but points to an alarming fatalism in its wider inferences. "Back to nature" is surely a false track, and to simulate a primaeval simplicity must lead to suffering and despair. Indeed, to look upon the world with innocent eyes may be easy once we have mastered the trick of shutting out our own multiplicity. In "Harry Haller's Records," which Hermann Hesse has given us in his book *Steppenwolf,* this attitude of innocence is exposed to wise stricture:

He who sentimentally sings of blessed childhood is thinking of the return to nature and innocence and the origin of things, and has quite forgotten that these blessed children are beset with conflict and complexities and capable of all suffering.

There is, in fact, no way back either to the wolf or to the child. From the very start there is no innocence and no singleness. Every created thing, even the simplest, is already guilty, already multiple. It has been thrown into the muddy stream of being and may never more swim back again to its source. The way to innocence, to the uncreated and to God leads on, not back, not back to the wolf or to the child, but ever further into sin, ever deeper into human life. . . . Instead of narrowing your world and simplifying your soul, you will at last take the whole world into your soul, cost what it may, before you are through and come to rest.[7]

[6] *"Von der Freundlichkeit der Welt,"* Gedichte I, p. 58, reads in the last verse:

> "Von der Erde voller kaltem Wind
> Geht ihr all bedeckt mit Schorf und Grind.
> Fast ein jeder hat die Welt geliebt
> Wenn man ihn zwei Hände Erde gibt."

[7] *Steppenwolf* (New York: Ungar, 1957), pp. 86–87. This ever deeper

The way of reconciliation must penetrate more deeply into human nature, into its guilt as well as its innocence; and we must learn to treat the givenness of life not as a spur to our opposing forces, but as a challenge to mingle good with evil, so that both interpenetrate, the good transforming the evil, as environment in its entirety is absorbed into ourselves.

In contrast to Brecht's "serene acquiescence" in the natural order is the attitude of the nature-mystic [8] Richard Jefferies, whose rapture in the contemplation of the world fails to dissolve his feelings of the hostility of nature, which he felt to be totally indifferent to the lot of man.

There is nothing human in the whole round of nature. All nature, all the universe that we can see, is absolutely indifferent to us, and except to us human life is of no more value than grass. If the entire human race perished at this hour, what difference would it make to the earth? What would the earth care? As much as for the extinct dodo, or for the fate of the elephant now going? . . . a great part, perhaps the whole, of nature and of the universe is distinctly anti-human. The term inhuman does not express my meaning, anti-human is better; outre-human, in the sense of beyond, outside, almost grotesque in its attitude towards, would nearly convey it. Everything is anti-human.[9]

progression into human life is indicated also by Miguel de Unamuno in *The Tragic Sense of Life* (New York: Dover, 1954), p. 264, where his word "eternalize" means "to infuse with love." "Everything deserves to be eternalized, absolutely everything, even evil itself, for that which we call evil would lose its evilness in being eternalized, because it would lose its temporal nature."

[8] Nature-mystics have sometimes assumed that "nature" and "God" are interchangeable, and have spoken of their experience as "pantheistic." "Pantheism" means literally "all-God-ism," but the experience of union with the natural world may more properly be described as "panenhenism," "all-in-one-ism." Richard Jefferies, who rejected the idea of a personal God, exemplifies this relationship with nature.

[9] *The Story of My Heart* (London: Longmans, Green, 1920), pp. 63–64.

Despite this harsh interpretation of the natural world, however, Jefferies was deeply stirred by his environment in town and country. Enraptured by the hostile earth, and "all the designless, formless chaos of chance-directed matter," he felt a seep sense of kinship with it. Earth, sky and sun, he wrote,

gave me inexpressible delight, as if they embraced and poured out their love upon me. It was I who loved them, for my heart was broader than the earth; [10]

so that whereas his judgement of the earth's grotesqueness might have locked and frozen its springs of nourishment against him, his love of the world kept them open. He communed with the inner meaning of objects, with their essences which he himself projects into them and draws from them. And if Jefferies does not answer fully von Weizsäcker's question about his Icelandic crystal, "How do I really know that my psychological relation to this crystal does not belong to it as an objective property?" Jefferies certainly believes that the material world is permeated with subtle energy, "more subtle than electricity," and has the power of producing sympathetic reactions in the human mind.

Beyond this poetic and mystical appreciation of the world in its totality, there are experiences of a different order which also evoke an acceptance of the whole. The fact that the following examples are drawn from fiction does not make them fictitious in the sense of arbitrary invention. Rather are they deeply lived inward events which, given the form of tangible experiences, bear their own weight of authority. In *Free Fall*, William Golding's character Sammy Mountjoy, with a detachment born of proxim-

[10] *Ibid.*, p. 79.

ity with death, and luminously sane, emerges from the darkness of torture to find his prison camp, and indeed all things, shining "with the innocent light of their own created nature."

I looked up beyond the huts and the wire, I raised my dead eyes, desiring nothing, accepting all things and giving all created things away. . . . Beyond them the mountains were not only clear all through like purple glass, but living. They sang and were conjubilant. They were not all that sang. Everything is related to everything else and all relationship is either discord or harmony. The power of gravity, dimension and space, the movement of the earth and sun and unseen stars, these made what might be called music and I heard it.[11]

And Mountjoy professes utter amazement to discover that the jubilant interrelatedness of the world is sustained by "a kind of vital morality":

not the relationship of a man to remote posterity nor even to a social system, but the relationship of individual man to individual man.[12]

This he regarded as a precious element in any new world, though modern man had dismissed it: scientifically because it did not yield to quantitative analysis, and politically because it caught no votes. Mountjoy's vision is not vegetative like Brecht's nor filled with yearning like that of Jefferies,[13] but contains an introspectiveness illuminated by the glory of the world itself. This glory however, reveals an inwardness of the most sombre hue, for the human nature he finds inhabiting the centre of his awareness "could be likened to nothing but the most loathsome substances that man knows,

[11] *Free Fall* (New York: Harcourt, Brace, 1960), pp. 186–87.

[12] *Ibid.*, p. 189.

[13] *The Story of My Heart*, p. 117: ". . . my life is burning in me. The soul throbs like the sea for a larger life. No thought which I have ever had has satisfied my soul."

or perhaps the most loathsome and abject creatures." [14] At the heart of his acceptance of the world in its totality lies an acknowledgment of the multiplicity of his own person, uncovered in the agony of torture.

Albert Camus faces the challenge of the totality of nature in a situation of extreme stress and strain. His response occurs in *The Plague* and is expressed in the words and humanity of Christian and agnostic alike, for Father Paneloux's bold and muscular faith is matched by the sensitive humanitarianism of Jean Tarrou, who recognises, beyond its physical symptoms, the inwardness and universality of the plague, and lives responsibly and vigilantly beneath its lethal shadow.

In the need to face honestly the terrible implications of a child's agony, Paneloux's faith reaches a crisis in which he must either "believe everything or deny everything." He is reported as saying in his second sermon that:

God had vouchsafed to His creatures an ordeal such that they must acquire and practise the greatest of all virtues: that of the All or Nothing . . . the total acceptance of which he had been speaking was not to be taken in the limited sense . . . of mere resignation or even of that harder virtue, humility. It involved humiliation, but a humiliation to which the person humiliated gave full assent. [15]

Paneloux considered it wrong to say, *"This* I understand, but *that* I cannot accept." Humiliated by the mystery of evil he was ready to accept it in its direct forms, and because it was humiliating, to manoeuver himself into a position from which it would be possible to introduce into evil that good which lay within human power. This positive choice was his alternative to denying everything. In the inescapable di-

[14] *Free Fall,* p. 189.
[15] *The Plague* (London: Penguin, 1960), p. 184.

lemma presented to the Christian by evil, Paneloux chose an "active fatalism"; consenting to all the possibilities of evil as of God, he poured into them what skill and comfort lay at his command, thus keeping alive his faith rather than abandoning it, and willing the divine will rather than hating God.[16]

Jean Tarrou's language is different, but his attitude and behaviour are commensurable with those of Father Paneloux. Tarrou knows positively "that each of us has the plague within him; no one, no one on earth is free from it," and that "on this earth there are pestilences and there are victims, and it's up to us, so far as possible, not to join forces with the pestilences." [17]

Sensing the unity of man's inward and outward life, Tarrou combines his struggle on behalf of the plague victims with the constant exercise of will-power and imagination in order to avoid that careless moment in which he might breathe infection upon others, and attempts to follow "the path of sympathy" towards the kind of humanity which has been called "secular sanctity."

[16] In a letter to the Rev. J. M. Perrin contained in her book *Waiting on God* (London: Fontana, 1959), pp. 13–14, Simone Weil considers the problem of complete conformity to the will of God. She believes that all the events and situations not directly dependent upon us, that is to say, "all the accomplished facts in the whole universe at the moment, and everything which is happening or going to happen later beyond our reach" comes about in accordance with the will of God, "without any exception." In this domain that is independent of us she says "we must love absolutely everything, as a whole and in each detail, including evil in all its forms; notably our own past sins, in so far as they are past (for we must hate them in so far as their root is still present), our own sufferings, past, present, and to come, and—what is by far the most difficult—the sufferings of other men in so far as we are not called upon to relieve them." In this way we are to feel the reality and presence of God through all external things, without exception, "as clearly as our hand feels the substance of paper through the pen-holder and the nib."

[17] *The Plague*, p. 207.

152

Thus far, then, the "acceptance of the world" in its totality abandons the passivity with which the idea of acceptance is sometimes associated, and not only recognises the sheer existence of things, but also their power to enlarge and deepen our self-awareness, and so to function positively in the processes of our becoming. ("The sufferings of children were our bread of affliction, but without this bread our souls would die of hunger." [18])

Simultaneously, acceptance indicates a quality of vision altogether involving the beholder: a vision so disciplined by attentiveness and loyalty to relationships and things as to grant each passing moment the highest significance, and so marked by courage and audacity as to accept the multiplicity and paradox of oneself and the world.

These qualities of vision come to life in Nietzsche, whose boundless capacity for pain and courageous endurance of loneliness issue in a triumphant affirmation of life in its entirety. Nietzsche's remarkable honesty, coupled with his innermost desire and profoundest need to apprehend the truth of this world, leads him step by step into the abyss. Reasoning without appeal to the otherworldly he dismantles the metaphysical framework of life, demythologises man's aesthetic, ethical and religious experiences, proposing completely natural explanations for them, so that the most exalted states of mind are attributable only to instincts. From this outer world he turns to explore man's inwardness and the compensatory world of dreams to reveal those needs and desires which, cleansed and refreshed during sleep, continue to exert their power over our waking life through the closed hatches of our suppression. If rational thinking reflects nonrational forces, who can trust his intel-

[18] Father Paneloux's reported sermon, in *The Plague*, p. 185.

lectual conscience? And if knowledge is conditioned by the merely instrumental role of the intellect, not even science can liberate us from errors and phantasies! If the intellectual conscience itself is born of utilitarian considerations and traces its ancestry to motives of benefit and injury, pleasure and pain, what evidence can it produce of its ability to ascertain the truth? And if life be fundamentally resolved into terms of inclination and aversion, why should we assume that the world is so ordered as to be tolerable to us? There is no pre-established harmony between the promotion of truth and the welfare of mankind. And can one consciously remain in untruth?

At the point where his intellectual conscience, already prepared to kill its immediate ancestry, is poised to commit suicide, Nietzsche collided with the forces of ascending life within himself, and his midnight depths are tinged with the pallid light of dawn. Looking beyond conscious reasoning and moral choosing he saw these activities simply as signs of those deeper forces of life, not under our conscious control but to which we nevertheless belong and are subject. His pessimism becomes joyful wisdom in the recognition that life itself bears us along towards its goal; our argumentation, valuing and rationalising are circuitous routes to an end already decreed by life itself. In his nihilistic descent the will to truth appeared as destructive to life; in the light of a new dawn he views it as the servant of profounder physiological demands and of the hidden forces which comprise the world. Our conscious intellectual struggles are a roundabout way of obeying life's decree.

So the dark loneliness of his intellectual struggle was pregnant with this wisdom, and towards the end of his book which heralds the dawn, in an aphorism entitled "Circuitous Routes," he enquires:

154

Where does all this philosophy mean to end with its circuitous routes? Does it do more than transpose into reason, so to speak, a continuous and strong impulse . . . for all the things which are suited to my own personal taste? a philosophy which is in the main the instinct for a personal regimen . . . and takes the circuitous routes of my head to persuade me to it! There are many other and certainly more lofty philosophies, and not only such as are more gloomy and pretentious than mine—and are they perhaps, taking them as a whole, nothing but intellectual circuitous routes of the same kind of personal impulses?—In the meantime I look with a new eye upon the mysterious and solitary flight of a butterfly high on the rocky banks of the lake where so many plants are growing: there it flies hither and thither, heedless of the fact that its life will last only one more day, and that the night will be too cold for its winged fragility. For it, too, a philosophy might be found, though it might not be my own.[19]

Thus Nietzsche comes to regard himself, not over against nature but as a part of it; mind is now one with body, no longer a master but a servant; for there are no eternal facts and no absolute truths; the sovereign purposes of the world are hidden in the recesses of the Unconscious. His good news is to accept the world in its totality, together with man—even in his irresponsibility; we are to be like those geniuses whom he describes as "possessors of the pure and purifying eye which . . . looks out upon the world as upon a God whom it loves." [20] His formula is *amor fati,* love of "that which has been spoken by the gods," and against the dualisms of what should be preserved and what destroyed he proclaims the doctrine of Eternal Recurrence, which not only places a mark of eternity upon everything, but also seals his sense of its acceptance.

This joyful wisdom augments the beauty of the world.

[19] Nietzsche, *Dawn of Day,* in Levy, *op. cit.,* IX, pp. 385–86.
[20] *Ibid.,* p. 348.

Those who reserve their veneration and feelings of happiness for works of fancy and imagination may well be disenchanted when they leave these romantic realms for the world of ordinary events and things; those who judge the world on moral grounds will find it cruel or disgusting. But those who, from one viewpoint or another, see reality as ugly

overlook the fact that the knowledge of even the ugliest reality is beautiful, and that the man who can discern much and often is in the end very far from considering as ugly the main items of that reality, the discovery of which has always inspired him with the feeling of happiness.

Is there anything 'beautiful in itself'? The happiness of those who can recognize augments the beauty of the world, bathing everything that exists in a sunnier light: discernment not only envelops all things in its own beauty, but in the long run permeates the things themselves with its beauty—may ages to come bear witness to the truth of this statement! [21]

Thus in his pilgrimage Nietzsche is borne up from nihilistic depths to a joyous affirmation of the world. Having dismantled the entire metaphysical framework of existence he establishes that there is nothing good or beautiful, sublime or evil in itself, but that these epithets represent states of human awareness which we bestow as predicates upon the external world. If then it be man who must make things true and beautiful, Nietzsche will exercise a "discernment" which envelops and finally permeates with its beauty the whole of creation, and love becomes a bridge to the total acceptance of the world.

[21] *Ibid.*, pp. 381–82.

9

Love of All Things

He called all creatures by the name of brother, and in a surpassing manner, of which other men had no experience, he discerned the hidden things of creation with the eye of the heart, as one who had already escaped into the glorious liberty of the children of God.

> *Thomas of Celano* [1]

In love we do not discover values, we discover in its movement that everything is more valuable.

> *Karl Jaspers* [2]

COMPARED WITH the "active fatalism" that desires to take the whole world into itself, infusing it wherever possible with love, is the religious view associated with the Orient, which regards our present existence as coextensive with pain. It sees man's task as one of reducing the reality of the world to a shadowy status, and ultimately of escaping from its trammels and from all that is individual and personal, in the extinction of the self. This movement from personal identification with the mass-misery of all things to complete estrangement from them rests upon a view which envisages the world as a living whole, permeated by a unitary life.

In Western antiquity, particularly among the Greeks, the sense of the undivided total life of a single world was more

[1] *The Lives of St. Francis* (London: Methuen, 1908), "The First Life of St. Francis," p. 79.

[2] *Psychologie der Weltanschauungen* (5th ed.; Berlin: Springer-Verlag, 1960), p. 124: *"Es sind nicht 'Werte' die entdeckt würden in der Liebe, sondern in der Bewegung der Liebe wird alles wertvoller."*

157

active and positive than its oriental counterpart. It contained more joy than sorrow. In contrast with the oriental sense of the evil of the world we may set the Scholastic axiom that *"omne ens est bonum"* which permeates the basic notions of the Western world, and bears some of the flavour of man's communion with all things in God. But the detached admiration of the Greeks for nature, coupled with the Old Testament suggestion that nature is at the *service* of man, eventually made for a superior and condescending attitude in Western man towards animal, vegetable and inorganic life. This process received further impetus from the Christian affirmation of God as the invisible, spiritual "Lord and Maker" of the world, under whose hand nature became less animate and less alive, while by the same token, man as a spiritual being acquired such precedence over nature that his feelings of unity with nature have in general been branded as paganism during the Christian centuries. The doctrine of the Incarnation and the lengthy discussion of the two natures in Christ seemed not to fertilise an awareness of the possibility that human nature might be rooted inextricably in the larger reality of nature itself, though man's ties of brotherhood with plant and animal, wind and weather, were briefly but brilliantly revived in the Franciscan movement of the thirteenth century.

Christian man has struggled to disengage himself emotionally from nature in the name of the transcendent God and on behalf of his own immortal soul. If not his divorce, then his "legal separation" from nature was effected in order to concentrate energy upon a love of persons in accord with the love of Jesus Christ; but this emphasis drew from him the view that nature is a lifeless instrument of man's "spiri-

158

tual" existence, and that man himself in his "fleshly" capacity represented a force running counter to the spirit. This attitude to nature showed itself first in asceticism of the body and then in the technological conquest of nature. The materialising of nature and the spiritualising of man are facets of one movement in which nature and man are forced apart. Man's destiny has been theologically expressed in terms of the doctrine of the *imago Dei,* man's "fall," and his subsequent adoption, through Christ, into the family of God the Father and Creator, but in such a way that only human beings are interrelated. The works of nature were not regarded as man's kindred; they were subservient, and over them man exercised the rights of a lord and master. F. W. Schelling, who sought to revive the animism of antiquity, argued that the Christian habit of mind, particularly in its thinking about God, could not avoid conceiving of the world as a "dead aggregate." In his lectures on monotheism Schelling asks:

Is it not clear that at the same time and in the same degree to which nature was freed from divinity, it deteriorated to the condition of a sheer, dead aggregate, and lively monotheism evaporated to leave a vacant, indefinite theism without content? [3]

In the nature and development of the Christian sacraments we do find preserved a vital identification of Christ with matter; his flesh and blood "appear" under forms of bread and wine, but these have come to be virtually the only natural substances which allow of that kind of "union"

[3] *Schellings Werke,* VI (München: C. H. Beck'sche Verlagsbuchhandlung, 1959), pp. 360–61: *"Oder liegt es nicht am Tage, dass zugleich und in demselben Verhältniss, in welchem die Natur immer mehr jeder Göttlichkeit entledigt, zum blossen, todten Aggregat herabsank, auch der lebendige Monotheismus sich immer mehr in einen leeren, unbestimmten, inhaltslosen Theismus verflüchtigte?"*

that the ancients were able to establish with the entire world. Henri de Lubac hints that there are "rich resources of scripture and the great doctors on the subject of man's solidarity with the universe," [4] yet despite these literary allusions Christianity, inspired with a compassion for all mankind, seldom directs this compassion towards the natural world, but has tended, rather, to regard it as apparatus provided for man's use during his probation here!

The remarkable exception to this general attitude is that of St. Francis of Assisi, whom Max Scheler describes in his work on *The Nature of Sympathy* as "one of the greatest artificers of the spirit in European history." [5] Francis sought to unite within a single lifestream the compassion of Christianity and the animistic sense of union with the natural world. He addressed sun and moon, fire and water, plants and animals of many descriptions as his "brothers" and "sisters," and widened the circle of love for God and our neighbour to include the lower orders of nature. And this he did in such a way as not to degrade man but to raise the world of nature into new light and glory.

Christians from earliest times were aware, in some sense or other, that who Christ was and what he had done affected the entire world; but in what way this cosmic dimension of his person and work should impinge, through them, upon their immediate physical environment, they did not understand. Those who might have reinterpreted in

[4] *Catholicism* (London: Burns and Oates, 1950), p. xi. Irenaeus is an excellent example. In his *Adversus haereses* the fifth book is chiefly concerned with the redemption of man's physical body, and indeed, the whole material order. The Eucharist shows that the material world is capable of receiving spiritual benefit, while Christ's bodily resurrection and ascension indicate that the material world will be caught up finally in redemption.

[5] (New Haven: Yale University Press, 1954), p. 87.

their scholarly pursuits the cosmic eschatology of the Bible were either impeded by powerful influences which depreciated matter or were imprisoned within a conservatism which preferred simply to reassert the physical references without deducing their immediate importance.[6]

The natural objects and processes to which the Gospels refer, including those which reveal the sensitivity of Jesus to the natural world, seem only to function in a parabolic way by showing what ties should bind human beings together and what relationships exist between them and God. That birds are fed and flowers clothed by God indicates their relation with divinity apart from man, yet the Gospels enjoin no duty to love nature as such, and envisage no overflowing love in the direction of the natural world. God's care for his creatures accentuates man's reluctance to trust in divine providence; the appeal to human kindness in the rescue of a stranded sheep aims at evoking such compassion for a man in distress as to sweep aside Sabbath restrictions upon physical movement, for "How much then is a man better than a sheep?" (Matt. 12:12, AV)

St. Francis is different. He does not speak of nature in this scriptural fashion, but expresses feelings of direct relatedness with all creatures. Water may remind him of baptism, and lambs of the Lamb of God, but these formally religious associations break down in face of the multiplicity of creatures with whom he expressed his joy. In the second of *The Lives of St. Francis*, Thomas of Celano says that, "Everywhere he followed the Beloved by the traces He has impressed on all things; he made for himself of all

[6] Cf. A. D. Galloway, *The Cosmic Christ* (London: Nisbet, 1951), pp. 121–23, where the author summarises his argument by showing the limited use made of the implications of the Gospel.

things a ladder whereby he might reach the Throne. He embraced all things with an unheard-of rapture of devotion, speaking to them of the Lord and exhorting them to praise Him.' [7] He visualises the world neither as functioning mechanically in the absence of God nor as equated with God, but as participating in the reality of God. In this regard Max Scheler notes that

what is really new and unusual in St. Francis's emotional relationship to Nature, is that natural objects and processes take on an expressive significance of *their own,* without any parabolic reference to man or to human relationships generally. Thus sun, moon, wind and so on, which have no need whatever of benevolent or compassionate love, are greeted in heartfelt recognition as brother and sister. All created things are taken in their metaphysical contiguity (man being also included), to be *immediately* related to their Creator and Father as self-subsistent beings having, even in relation to man, a *quite intrinsic value of their own.* [8]

St. Francis' intuitive understanding of the relationship among nature, man and God is fuller and richer than that feeling for the world which we noted as finding a place in Christian Scripture. Natural objects participate in the being of God in a way that is not immediately evident in the Gospels. They point to God, not because men interpret them, or speak about them in parables in order to describe their relations with each other and with God, but simply because they are *there*. Again, as Scheler notes, St. Francis is opposed to the Scholastic understanding of nature as a hierarchy of being, but thinks of it as a living whole, manifesting from end to end the life of God. He rejoices in the "holiness" of everything. Further, he does not conceive of

[7] *The Lives of St. Francis,* p. 297.
[8] *The Nature of Sympathy,* p. 89.

God simply as Lord and Creator of the natural order, and Father of the human family alone. For him, God is the Father of all creatures as such, and by the grace of Christ they too become the objects of his love. This loving adoption of creatures into God's family means that the natural world enters into family relations with man. Thus St. Francis transcends the unilateral authority of man over nature, and in doing so he appeals to the Bible to authenticate his love of the natural world. On the face of it, we tend to agree that he read into the Scriptures a dimension of love which the writers themselves did not share. This may be so. But if Christ is God's *final* word, God's *télos* out of which our future grows, and therefore a seminal word, we must judge whether or not St. Francis realised the genuine implications of the fact of Christ. The remarkable circumstance in this connection is that his realisation of the life of God in nature did not volatilise his personal piety or corrupt his moral character. His rigorous imitation of Christ was not maintained in spite of his attitude to fellow creatures, but was rooted in it, while his humble following of Christ inspired his love of the natural world. On this account he has been described as embodying the most sublime example of a simultaneous inspiriting of life and enlivening of the spirit.

It was not within the vocation or the accomplishments of St. Francis to "ground" his rapturous vision of God and the natural world in theological formulae; others have undertaken this translation for him. It has been stated in the following terms:

Christ's supernatural act of redemption, though none the less an historical event, is at the same time an eternal miracle in the order of metaphysical reality, perpetuated in the Church and

163

her sacraments, and especially in the Eucharist, wherein God everlastingly takes flesh upon Him and is made man; a miracle which must serve as a pattern for the ideal of a moral and religious *Imitatio Christi,* extending to a complete identity of structure between the believer's personality and that of Christ. *At the same time . . .* this supernatural being and becoming also prefigures, in its innermost meaning, the continual life-giving incarnation of God the Father in *Nature*—an active continuance of creation, parallel to the sacrifice of Christ. Hence there is in truth but one divine life dwelling in all created things, and it is as forms of expression for this divine life, as "natural sacraments," so to speak, and as a system of real symbols pointing to God the Father, that they can and should be regarded by men.[9]

This family relationship between nature, man and God, which informs the vision of St. Francis, is more articulate than the unity indicated in phrases such as "the coinherence of matter and spirit" or "the interpenetration of matter and spirit." St. Francis addresses the natural world in terms of personal fellow feeling, which is the language of sympathetic insight and springs from his genius for devoting loving attention to the heart of all natural life. He does not simply recognise spirit in matter, but godlike life in all created things.

The triumph of natural science and a mechanistic view of the world contrive to make this personal appraisal of nature ridiculous and untenable, though perhaps generously permitted to poets and mystics. The bestowal of personal qualities upon creation by St. Francis is thought to be illusory, anthropomorphic, lacking in cognitive significance, and superseded by the disciplines of science linked with the concerns of humanism. A general love of mankind replaces the saint's love of everything immediate and universal, and this

[9] *Ibid.,* p. 91.

general love rests upon a social understanding of man, mechanically related to nature and estranged from God.

In exercising its special disciplines science excludes its feelings for nature, not because sympathetic identification with the world is illegitimate as a mode of participating in its life, but because one of the principles of selecting the data upon which the body of science may grow is the advancement of technical aims. The picture that science constructs of the world must be one which makes nature tractable and open to man's control. This attitude is a necessary element in our approach to the world, but does not rule out an emotional relationship which reflects the inwardness of things. Each view—the emotional and the technical—has its own proper existence, but not in isolation from the other; and the question of their relationship is one of the chief concerns of this enquiry.

The nonscientific, emotional regard for nature cannot be dismissed, for even a scientific approach to the world depends upon a relationship of some kind. Nature *only* shows positive "meaning" and "value" when we identify ourselves with it in one way or another. Without this relationship nature would not even be "worth" mastering! The assumption that the world is formally adapted to scientific exploitation seems meaningless unless it is born and nourished in some kind of *enthusiastic* association. Scientific endeavour, basing itself upon a one-sided conception of nature as a mere instrument of human domination, is caught up in programmes of destruction. A science of survival may pursue its disciplines only within the cultivation of human nature; it dare not implement exclusively those views of the world held by scientific experts, but must allow them to be modified and defined by a conception of life as a whole. It is

165

important to escape the view that the world is "an aggregation of movable quantities" (Scheler) and to promote man's native capacity for identifying himself with the life of the universe. This sense of unity with the world, analysed as an "empathic" projection of human emotion into plants, creatures and objects, is judged to be anthropomorphic in the sense of being a misapprehension of nature. We must set this judgement aside in favour of the view that man is a microcosm, an actual embodiment of the reality of existence in all its forms; he is *cosmomorphic* and possesses sources of insight into what is comprised in the nature of the world.

When we consider man's imperialistic acquaintance with nature, we see that it induced him to set up mechanical and organic conceptions of the universe as absolute principles, only to find himself uneasily cast off by nature. The inadequacy of these less-than-human principles of interpretation and behaviour were then supplemented with advice about love and forbearance towards plants and animals and our physical environment, not because the earth is kin to man, but simply because harshness and cruelty have a way of rebounding upon their perpetrators. At the other extreme, however, failure to ascribe intrinsic value to the world because of its unity with us permitted man to rape and destroy his natural resources, sometimes without a qualm; his love of humanity divorced from a sense of kinship with the world produced a form of "hatred" of humanity, for it set the achievement of maximum production and profit above man's skill, vitality and creative productivity; his failure to participate in the inwardness of things led to covetousness and the amassment of things.[10] In short, the

[10] Cf. Erich Fromm, *The Sane Society* (London: Routledge & Kegan Paul, 1956), pp. 120 ff.

ideal of dominating nature and those activities which serve such an end become meaningless when they cease to refer to man as a living creature and absorb him merely as a sentient part of themselves. This criticism, however, calls for an explanation of what is meant when we speak of man's identification or unity with the natural world. How may we identify ourselves with the life of the universe?

There is a sociology of knowledge informing the works of Max Scheler which deserves great attention. We contain within ourselves, he says, all the essential psychic structures developed in the course of evolution. The most primitive, undifferentiated, vital impulse, the only source of psychic energy throughout the evolutionary process, reaches into the highest forms of human life. This impulse (*Gefühls-drang*) is the power behind every activity, "even behind those on the highest spiritual level, and it provides the energy even for the purest acts of thought and the most tender expressions of good will." [11] There is no feeling, no perception and no idea into which this impulse does not enter.

> The force that through the green fuse drives the flower
> Drives my green age;
> . . . that drives the water through the rocks
> Drives my red blood; . . . .[12]

This same power also awakens us to "reality" by turning objects into "things that object"—by their very resistance to its movement. Man's cosmomorphic nature is the basis of Scheler's sociology of knowledge:

[11] Max Scheler, *Man's Place in Nature* (Boston: Beacon, 1961), p. 9.
[12] From *The Collected Poems* of Dylan Thomas (New York: New Directions, J. Laughlin, 1946), p. 10. Copyright 1939 by New Directions. Reprinted by permission of New Directions Publishing Corporation.

To all knowledge (indeed, to all intentional acts) there must correspond a being, and to all being a possible knowledge; similarly, to all loving and preferring there must correspond a value-fact (Wertbestand), and to every value-fact a loving and a preferring.[13]

And he explores the knowledge to which this community of feelings gives access. In *The Nature of Sympathy* Scheler makes a careful distinction between *Mitgefühl*, feeling with someone, and other attitudes which might easily be confused with it. His concept of sympathy must not be mistaken for mere understanding of another person's experience: that is to say, the situation in which we understand from a man's expressions and gestures just how he is feeling. Such understanding as this could be a constitutent of refined cruelty or sadism as well as of fellow feeling: "I can quite visualise your feelings, but I have no pity for you!" Nor is fellow feeling the same as emotional sharing or contagion as when panic sweeps through a crowd; it cannot be equated with the anguish of two parents who stand united in a community of feeling over the dead body of their child, for the bowed shoulders of their grief express one identical, inward sorrow. Nor is sympathy one of those strange processes known as "identifications" in which one person projects himself into the feelings and position of another, or allows the attitudes of another to absorb and dominate his own.

The sympathy which Scheler positively delineates is essentially one which preserves the distance and distinction

[13] *Vom Ewigen in Menschen*, I (Leipzig: Der Neue Geist Verlag, 1923), Part II, p. 139: *"Aller Erkenntnis (ja allen intentionalen Akten) muss ein Sein, allem Sein eine mögliche Erkenntnis entsprechen; analog allem Lieben und Vorziehen ein Wertbestand, jedem Wertbestand ein Lieben und Vorziehen."*

between persons. True fellow feeling is functional, and does not refer to the state of one's own feelings:

In commiserating with B, the latter's state of feeling is given as located entirely in B himself: it does not filter across into A, the commiserator, nor does it produce a corresponding or similar condition in A. It is merely 'commiserated with', not undergone by A as a real experience.[14]

We can sense the emotional states of others and really "suffer" with them or "rejoice" with them. Our rejoicing or suffering *with* them does not mean that we are joyful or sorrowful on their account, for that would be our own joy or sadness, taking root through infective propagation. Indeed, Scheler sets aside the theories which explain fellow feeling by saying that when we perceive the symptoms and occasioning circumstances of joy or sorrow in others, this has the effect either of evoking similar feelings which we have ourselves experienced, or of inducing us to imitate the symptoms we perceive. In place of this reasoning he says that "in true, unalloyed commiseration and rejoicing there is no state of sorrow or joy in oneself," [15] but a genuine outreaching and entry into another person and his individual situation, and authentic self-transcendence, so that genuine fellow feeling permits us to savour the joy or sadness of others without getting into their particular mood ourselves.

And when we ask how such knowledge of others is possible Scheler dismisses all those answers which depend upon inference or analogy and empathy. Our knowledge of others is not acquired by analogy, as when we deduce from another's facial expression which is known to us, what is going on inside him. Babies can grasp the meaning of facial

[14] *The Nature of Sympathy,* p. 41.
[15] *Ibid.,* p. 45.

expressions without the ability to make deductions. Even our adult deductions will not permit us to conclude that there are minds different from our own, only that there are minds identical with them. And if, instead of concluding from the configuration of the human features that people are angry, we *feel* ourselves into them and understand them by empathy, from this transference of our own lives on to those of others we could not deduce more than that our kind of awareness of life was reduplicated in others. However, these explanations and the questions they presuppose rest on the assumption that self-consciousness is in some way primary and antecedent to social consciousness, that we first know our own selves, then grope our way to a knowledge of others with the help of these theories. But life is *not* so ordered; it grants us knowledge of other minds prior to awareness of our own. We do not start with an "I," then enlarge it, so to speak, into "we." "We" is more primitive than "I," which seems to emerge by dissociation or withdrawal from a collective consciousness. We have direct access to other minds because to begin with—as children— other minds form as integral a part of our immediate experience as anything else in the world. We discover ourselves only by differentiating ourselves from the community of other minds in which we were originally immersed; our distinctness as persons emerges upon the fading yet enduring background of a consciousness which included the experiences of other people.[16] And Scheler remarks:

Given the range of emotional qualities of which man is intrinsically capable, and from which alone his own actual feelings are built up, he has an *equally innate* capacity for compre-

[16] Cf. C. H. Cooley, *Social Organization* (New York: Scribners, 1909), p. 5: "Self and society are twin-born, we know one as immediately as we know the other."

170

hending the feelings of others, even though he may never on any occasion have encountered such feelings (or their ingredients) in himself, as real unitary experiences.[17]

This community of feelings gives us *access* to our environment of people and things, but how can we *know* human beings and our surroundings? We know them by love and sympathy, for these are also among man's primal endowments: pure fellow feeling is an intrinsic characteristic of the human spirit, given to us to appreciate the worth of others in general. It is not the product of our acquaintances with people and their emotional states, nor do those limited acquaintances determine or limit its scope; they only assist with opportunities for its application and display.

In our egocentricity the world revolves about us as a shadowy existence whence people and things are called forth according to our wants, then permitted to recede into their indefinite background. Love and sympathy give life to this realm of "shades," and enable us to see that human beings, as persons, are as valuable as ourselves. For love and fellow feeling are emotions in the sense of movements which lead us out of and beyond ourselves (*ēmovēre* is "to move away"). But whereas sympathy is response to the experiences of others, love is the spontaneous motion which gives it range and depth and power. By its nature love penetrates the masks and concealments of men to the point of unknowability. And Scheler describes the "emotion" of love in the following way, carefully pointing out that

in love there is no attempting to fix an objective, no deliberate shaping of purpose, aimed at the higher value and its realization; *love itself, in the course of its own movement,* is what

[17] *The Nature of Sympathy*, p. 48.

brings about continuous *emergence* of ever higher value in the object—just as if it were streaming out from the object of its own accord, without any sort of exertion (even of wishing) on the part of the lover.[18]

The motion of love is sometimes explained by saying that it brings to light hitherto hidden values which were already present in the object, or that the moment of love itself is one in which these values are cultivated. While proverbially accepting blame for the imperceptions of the sensual impulses which accompany it, love indeed opens our eyes; but wide-awakeness is simply its consequence. Love is not "constantly prospecting" for higher values; such a search must betoken its absence, for concern with merits and dismissal of the failings in its object spell out illusion, and the nonappearance of "higher" values must then plunge us into disillusionment. But "love knows no end"; there is "no fading of its hope."

Love's opening of our vision must not be taken to mean that we grasp qualities in the object "higher" than those which close attention might discern. The higher values with which love is concerned are not previously given, but are present only in the moment of love.

Again, love has no stated values which its object "ought" to have, and does not therefore seek to change it. Seeing the faults, it loves them, and simply accepts *that which is given*. Even the phrase "loving things as they are" may be understood to mean loving them as possessing qualities we discern in them, or loving things through the medium of such qualities. But this is an ideal view which deprives love of its movement. If we say that love creates higher values, or that it moves towards them, this means that the one who is loving draws upon values within himself, and imputes

[18] *Ibid.*, p. 157.

them to the object of his attention. Unable to escape partiality for his own ideas he endows the object of his concern with qualities which it does not actually possess. The relationship then falls prey to our propensity for overvaluing the things we like, and "gaping" approval at them!

The inference Scheler draws, which sounds so strangely in modern ears, is that it is the "detached observer" who fails to recognise the individual values that belong to things. The detached observer is the *unemotional* onlooker, unable to move out of and beyond himself, who cannot accept the reality of the object, but in his isolation must project his own values on to it. It is love which sees the objective and the real, and accepts with clarity and openness the qualities pertaining to things themselves:

love is that movement wherein every concrete individual object that possesses value achieves the highest value compatible with its nature and ideal vocation; or wherein it attains the ideal state of value intrinsic to its nature.[19]

We must not then mistake this "emotional" understanding of love for a kind of mysticism. Mysticism is characterised by reflection and contemplation, by the negation of what is particular and individual, and by identity with the whole. Love as *emotion* is a movement which does not lose sight of concrete objects, but sees them within the totality of the world. Every single thing may become the object of this love. It is not given to us to grasp all things in literal objectivity, but we may look upon them as embedded in totality, and then they are, so to speak, shot through and through with light which streams from the whole, and they are bound up with it. Thus the totality of things reaches towards us in the particular object which shines in this light. In order to state this in Christian terms we should have to

[19] *Ibid.*, p. 161.

173

say that we see all things "in God," ἔνθεος, that is: "enthusiastically."

In addition to understanding things not as detached but as expressive of totality, we must recognise that the objects of love are enhanced in value *as they are loved*. Love is not a recognition of already existing values; love accepts things as they are; but in its own motion enhances the values it encounters in any concrete situation. For love, it is the individual instance or object which is adorned with totality, or, as William Blake's "Auguries of Innocence" suggest:

> To see a World in a Grain of Sand,
> And a Heaven in a Wild Flower.
> Hold Infinity in the palm of your hand
> And Eternity in an hour.[20]

From other standpoints a single object or instance is incidental. It is one among many. Knowledge regards it as an example, industry and commerce as a piece of material or a transaction; the historian finds it a significant detail; for the logician it is relative and finally incomprehensible. In short, from the empiricial viewpoint the individual object or instance is an inexhaustible infinity, but for love it is a grasped infinity which, as such, can never become the object of observation or knowledge. From the psychological point of view this grasped totality might even be judged to be an *idea* towards which our minds are always moving, but the unceasing movement of love cannot formulate or communicate directly that which is peculiar to itself. Unamuno depicts these relationships as follows:

[20] *The Complete Poetry and Selected Prose of John Donne and the Complete Poetry of William Blake* (New York: Random House, 1941), p. 597.

174

When I hear the groan of my neighbour, who to the eye is a form fitting other forms, I feel sorrow in my entrails, and through love, the revelation of *being*. Through love we get to things with our own *being*, not with the mind alone, we make them *fellow-beings*.[21]

It should also be clear that the movement of love does not represent specifically "human" characteristics. It relates spontaneously to whatever is of value. We love human beings for what they are, and rejoice in their enhancement; but we also love many kinds of things. Man is not the sole object of his love; in the language associated with Martin Buber, he may participate in I-Thou relationships with things as well as with people. If love extended only to whatever could be credited with "human" characteristics, its "pathetic" limitations would rest upon our ability to endow things with our own feelings. We would love things in order to promote our own existence—in estrangement from the world. Genuine love of the world means that the world is loved for its own sake; brutality towards it is then not wicked because it is regarded as an augury of brutality to man, but because it is wicked in itself. Genuine love of art, to take another example, expresses no gushing feeling which it then mistakes for values in the painting, but recognises there an extra human element which lifts man to a nobler humanity.

It is in this sense, then, as a movement which tends to enhance values, that love acquires significance as a creative force. It is in the realm of sensing and perceiving that love brings new values into existence, so that microcosmic man not only mirrors the world but also becomes the spearhead of its energies and an agent of its direction.

[21] *En torno al casticismo,* quoted in José Huertas-Hourda, *The Existentialism of Miguel de Unamuno* (Gainesville: University of Florida Press, 1963), p. 24.

175

10

The Inwardness and the Outwardness of Things

The religiously-minded can no longer turn their backs upon the natural world, or seek to escape from its imperfections in a supernatural world; nor can the materialistically-minded deny importance to spiritual experience and religious feeling.
Sir Julian Huxley [1]

To God all things are alive; O come let us adore Him.
Matins of the Dead [2]

THUS FAR we have sought to understand human beings as indissolubly and essentially one with their physical environment, and each person as an existential unity, extending into the surrounding world, but not internally divisible into body and soul. Man's environment has generally and usefully been defined as animate and inanimate, yet this division is arbitrary and may have no ultimate meaning. Man is not only dependent for his subsistence upon the physical universe, but its sensory bombardment of his person supplies him with data for an understanding of himself. His knowledge is relational in character. He may contemplate the world in the sensitiveness of his own person, and the world will reflect his interest (*inter esse*); it will present him with an image of his own being. If he speaks of the metaphysical *over against* physical reality, he also recalls that his

[1] Introduction to *The Phenomenon of Man* (London: Collins, 1959), p. 26.

[2] Words of the Invitatory, the Breviary of the Roman Catholic Church: *"Deum, cui omnia vivunt, venite adoremus."*

physical body evinces thinking and loving properties, and that the inseparability of brain and mind, of neural system and feeling, force him to accept these distinctions as complementary aspects of one existential whole. He views the spiritual and the material as the inwardness and the outwardness of things, devoid of life or meaning in themselves; and possibly, with multitudes of men, infers that there is indeed only one world, behind whose appearances nothing hides.

Within this self-awareness we have said that it is not unnatural that the whole earth should confront us as responsive, as *potentially* thinking and loving, and at certain levels as manifesting degrees of thought and love. In addition to remembering that nature is neither our enemy nor our servant, and that we ourselves *are* nature and the growing point of nature, the spearhead of creation, we have indicated the importance of absorbing wholly the fact that our roots delve far beneath the threshold of conscious reflection into evolutionary time, and that man is not a fixed quantity but a developing primate with millions of years of struggle and promise behind him. His long, hazardous journey may have begun in unconscious unity with the world, then crossed the bounds of self-awareness to drift into alienation from his home, but today he awakens startled by his predicament and the importance of some kind of reconciliation with the world, and is called to "come to himself." This is his task.

In the following chapters an attempt is made to delineate more sharply certain qualities of self-awareness, and therefore of world-awareness, which man's journey into the future seems to require of him at this particular time.

Nothing is static. Man is caught up in processes of

change and becoming in which his self-understanding penetrates and is answered by his environment; and in this dialectical encounter his conception of the world and grasp of his own nature are continually refashioned.

In order to sense this creative refashioning and to participate in the lively character of the world there seems to be no more promising ground of discovery or hidden wealth of resource than the Hebrew-Christian Scriptures. They reflect so descriptively and enter so deeply into the movement of universal life as to become veritable fountains of energy and inspiration for our human task. They elaborate themes of deliverance and reconciliation, rooted in historical events which are never permitted to become static, but continue to encounter and to be contemporary with succeeding generations. Unlike "beads strung on a chronological chain," the historical occasions they report and interpret become media of a particular quality of existence.

To account for this phenomenon of growth and contemporaneity, we may say that events in history are never quite objective, and always bear some of the characteristics of those who report them. The interpretation they receive enfolds their reporter's concern with life and his belief concerning its nature. The historian grapples with events at which he was not personally present; these he may understand by re-enacting in his own mind those earlier descriptions and processes of thought which have come down to him; so that to recreate the past it is necessary to stand within it in this sense, for it will not be genuinely interpreted from outside. Successive appraisals of past events shape themselves into tradition which becomes a kind of tangible memory spanning the gulf of time. By means of tradition we recall a once encountered reality and meet it afresh in ourselves. For remembering is not simply subjective reflection but a refashioning of the past. It is remembered *from* the present and brought up to date, covered with a new layer of interpretation, and given a new appearance. To remember the past is to recall events *from our point of view,* and this critical recollection is an expression of the past in new and lively shape. Thus history acquires contemporaneity and becomes an active force in the present time, till subsequent interpretation overlays and serenely integrates it into our cultural patrimony.

Biblical events have this character and refuse to be relegated to the past; within Christian tradition they have acquired a quality of reality to which changing historical situations have given fresh forms and content through the centuries. Rising generations tend to feel that their religious traditions are played out. In our own time it is widely held that those forces encapsuled in the Bible have now largely spent themselves, and that biblical insights no longer penetrate life as it is lived and understood. However, the value of biblical revelation will rest upon the depths of existence to which it reaches, while its "irrelevance" may be determined by unawareness of these depths in any age.

The Bible records certain determinative events which it then allows to grow by virtue of its basic modes of thought and concepts of life. The following chapters seek to interpret those elements in the traditions which relate to human beings and things from that understanding of man and his physical environment which we have sought in previous chapters to describe. Our concepts of the nature of the physical world and the significance of man have undergone considerable change in modern times, yet the biblical tradition, if addressed from our present-day *Weltanschauung,* may shine back with a light more penetrating and healing than that which now illumines our way. If the biblical past can still relate itself constructively to the present, it may become formative for the future; but this is not simply a matter of uncovering biblical elements of concordance with scientific vision, but of discovering their inwardness in order to touch the sources of life.

Martin Luther twice crossed the Swiss Alps without allowing their beauty, so far as we know, to penetrate his artistic soul; and it was left to Jean Jacques Rousseau to make this aesthetic discovery in which multitudes have subsequently shared. The appreciation of nature, however, is not a phenomenon of modern times alone, for the Hebrew conception of the natural world not only provides colour and material for narrative, but also shapes the imagery and inspires the vocabulary of the Bible.

The love-lyrics of the Song of Solomon, to take a notable example, are couched in descriptions of natural beauty, and the human qualities of the lovers themselves are presented in terms of plants, animals, trees, perfumes, birds, precious stones and metal, architecture and contours of the landscape. The picture of the young man is painted in these colours:

My beloved is all radiant and ruddy, distinguished among ten thousand.
His head is the finest gold; his locks are wavy, black as a raven.
His eyes are like doves beside springs of water, bathed in milk, fitly set.
His cheeks are like beds of spices, yielding fragrance.
His lips are lilies, distilling liquid myrrh.
His arms are rounded gold, set with jewels.
His body is ivory work, encrusted with sapphires.
His legs are alabaster columns, set upon bases of gold.

180

His appearance is like Lebanon, choice as the cedars.
His speech is most sweet, and he is altogether desirable.
This is my beloved, and this is my friend,
O daughters of Jerusalem.[3]

This aesthetic appreciation of nature envelops a sense of
wonder before the mystery and incomprehensibility of the
natural world, the forces which sustain it, the limits of the
cloud-wrapped ocean, the functions and behaviour of soil
and water, the dimensions of earth and the movements of
celestial bodies. The intricacy of nature, the habits of
animals and birds and the wisdom portrayed in their survival evoke the same *mysterium tremendum* (Job, chaps.
38 ff.).

But Hebrew men, like other men, could not permanently
live with the nonrational and mysterious without visualising
for themselves a rational order in things. A psalmist (Ps.
104) has been said to provide "the best picture of Nature as
a going concern" (H. Wheeler Robinson), and to a prophet
it was given to instruct us most clearly in the sociology of
nature:

I will answer the heavens,
and they shall answer the earth;
and the earth shall answer the grain, the wine, and the oil;
and they shall answer Jezreel.[4]

This ordered world of interrelated creatures and things is
not held together by "natural law," but is animated, ruled
and sustained by the "breath of Yahweh." And when we
turn from the phenomenological aspects of existence to the
inwardness of things, and from the immediate, sensory
impact of environment to consider what men thought about

[3] Song of Sol. 5: 10–16 (rsv).
[4] Hos. 2: 21–22 (rsv).

the material world, the biblical writers display an awareness of its nature which even now we may come to consider worthy of helping to shape our own relations with things. For they regarded the earth as alive, and acknowledged no fundamental distinction between the psychic and the corporeal, and between what we choose to call the "organic" and the "inorganic." Everything is a manifestation of life; the earth has its nature, makes itself felt, and demands respect; the very stones are alive; death is not antithetical to life, but is a phase of life.

This attitude has been thought, perhaps hastily, to embody a "prelogical mentality," yet Old Testament writers have no difficulty in distinguishing between the physical and metaphysical aspects of existence; but they believed in a unity of life which allowed of no separation between the material and the spiritual as *fundamental* forms of existence. For them, soul and body are *not* united; body *is* soul in its outwardness, and soul *is* body in its inwardness.

The total personality is operative in any one aspect or part of the whole, so that various parts of the body comprise psychical as well as physical properties; that is to say: man's consciousness is diffused throughout his person. The condition of the psalmist's life may be tested by the state of his kidneys, and Job's palate may pronounce upon perversity!

> Who hath put wisdom in the inward parts?
> or who hath given understanding to the heart? [5]

In contrast, therefore, with the mental habit which dissociates ideas from things, the Hebrews found it more natural

---

[5] *Job* 38: 36 (AV). Compare with this K. Stern, J. B. Boulanger and Sheena Cleghorn "The Semantics of Organ Language" *The American Journal of Psychiatry,* Vol. 106, No. 11 (May, 1950), describing idioms in which nouns for organs and verbs for organ functions express complex emotional processes.

to think descriptively and pictorially, linking firmly with ideas the objects, movements and sensory data of their environment. And unlike our predominant habit of analysis, of breaking up wholes into parts, they envisaged phenomena as participating in wholes. Man himself is thinking and feeling flesh, blood and bone. In trying to describe their view in our terms we might say that a man is insouled body and enfleshed soul, except that the Hebrew word *nephesh,* often translated "soul" and represented here by "a man," does not carry the fractional connotation to which "soul" is reduced in our minds by *association with* the body. *Nephesh* frequently expresses "life," but again without bearing the abstract sense which may lie hidden within our use of the word. The psalmist's cry for deliverance of soul is a spontaneous prayer that he himself be saved from death (Ps. 6:4).

Phrases describing the soul's departure at death and its return at life's renewal must not be understood as the severance of soul from body but, rather, as a diminishing or revival of man's total life; for a soul may be nourished physically and survive, while the dead are still "the weak." A corpse is a soul, "living and partly living"!

So, because the Hebrews understood consciousness to be distributed throughout the body, it was possible to conceive of psychical qualities in the natural world. After all, our bodies are the one part of nature of which we have an inside view, and the body seemed to show how nature felt and acted when viewed from within. It seemed natural to extend this awareness to the external world, to view environment anthropomorphically, as thoroughly animated, capable of fellow feeling with man, and capable of obedience to its sustaining depth of force.

Therefore, *nephesh* is not peculiarly human; there is no

183

ultimate division between human and animal *nephesh;* life and sensibility extend through the animal kingdom into the world of objects. Perhaps on account of the volatile nature of their contents, perfume bottles are "houses of the soul" (Isa. 3:20), and if mountains shake and trees "clap their hands" these personal propensities of a glad earth are more than poetry; they betoken an intrinsic connection between man and the earth, understood by analogy. And this relationship may be described as *living* because men visualised their surroundings as sharing in their own psychic nature.

In Israelite understanding man's individuality does not stop short at his physical exterior; his personality, unbounded by his bodily presence, extends into other persons and things regarded by the analytical mind as separate from him. A man's vital power bears not only the marks of his own character, but embraces also his relatives and property. If men are to be put to death their immediate relatives and possessions perish with them (cf. Num. 16:1–35; Josh. 7:24–25), yet this apparently wholesale carnage, on the understanding of extended personality, is unfortunately not without its *raison d'être.*

More positively stated, nothing in itself is lifeless; all is therefore susceptible to the force and content of *nephesh.* Objects share the qualities of their possessors; and to make a gift is to give something of oneself. More broadly speaking, the living earth is intimately connected with its inhabitants, whose personal life is reflected in the conditions of the impressionable soil and the forms of life it sustains. Earth's relationship to men is not that of a dead mass to living beings, but as partner in a covenant relationship not invariably dominated from the human side. The positive strength of life, the power to thrive and accomplish one's task, is called "blessing," while its opposite, "the curse," spells dissolution of soul. The land shares man's blessing and curse, responding bounteously to strength and kindness, but not suffering exhaustion without giving the appearance of a wilderness. And when, at seven-year intervals, its life becomes inviolate, this is not that it may lie fallow, but that it may become free, a no-man's land, pursuing its own nature. Man and earth are a psychic community; they are the constituents of personal life (Job 31:38–40).

The most immediate extension of *nephesh* occurs by word of mouth. The close connection between soul and that which is effected by it presupposes the power of the word: a force not wholly material as though a spoken word were a missile launched, nor yet an undifferentiated quantum of energy, but *essentially* powerful in a milieu capable of response by virtue of the same basic soul-quality.

Nephesh is characterized by its "fleshly" constituent (*basar*); it is not in itself an ontological substance, but has reality in localized, material, corporeal being. In man it does not operate with uniform strength, but depends upon the occasion and degree to which he "puts his heart into it." A man's name is the immediate bearer of his *nephesh;* his words of blessing augment life; his curses undo it. For when his *nephesh* is a totality which extends and moves out into space, thinking is not separate from speech, nor speaking from doing. Images of the memory press towards action; and words, in order to escape vanity, issue in event. Thinking is not pure theory, nor knowledge mere recognition. Concrete problems require more than abstract solutions and yield only to those whose shape is association, action and the appropriation of living wholes, and whose *modus vivendi* is that of intimacy, participation, fellow feeling, love.

This relationship of inwardness to outwardness is char-

185

acterised in Hebrew language by the absence of a word to represent a material thing. Things are sometimes referred to as means of action or objects of desire, but these designations still bear marks of human preference and motive; for the Hebrews, a thing is principally *dabhar,* a word.

In English a *thing* means any action, speech or thought with which we are concerned; it is any object of perception or knowledge; it is both idea and event. But our sense of discontinuity between thinking and doing makes us judge of this usage as ambiguous. The Hebrews find no ambiguity here: idea, word and event are a continuous whole. Abraham's returning servant recounts "all the words he had done" (Gen. 24:66). His adventurous journey in its entirety is comprised of *words!* Things are not objects in space; they are words! Things are not inflexibly *there,* but only changeably so! For they are directly and continuously related to man. Descriptions of earth in terms of motion and energy, the skipping mountains and their trembling foundations are more than poetic images of seismic phenomena and express a lively earth related to living man. *Dabhar,* or "word," comprises all: thoughts, words, deeds and concrete objects; while nonbeing, or nothingness, is explained by *lo-dabhar:* that which is "not-word." And between these extremes, couched within that unity of word and deed represented by *dabhar,* was a sense of counterfeit language: men recognised the word which lacked the strength of accomplishment, and deemed only the *effective* word to be the venture of *nephesh.* But the effective word could create or destroy in accordance with its character.

So the liveliness of *nephesh* becomes *dabhar;* its strength and quality pass into speech and action; its embryo is articulate energy: the notion of being behind and pressing for-

186

ward, and so, perhaps, of pressing words one after another into existence. In the realm of speech *dabhar* easily relates to "the idea behind it," and in that of action, to those forces and circumstances of which the event was a culmination. Events germinate in background words.

Thus *dabhar* contains and unfolds the essence of things; and when it appears as *logos* (as in the Septuagint), the Greek heritage [6] of this later form may heighten the intelligibility of the word, but does not staunch its Semitic flow of power. For in the prophetic tradition of Israel, the word which appeared as vision and action, poetry, prose and pun, and was understood to be an outpouring of the life of the speaker, acquired still deeper significance in the exercise of its prophetic function. The prophet became the spokesman of Yahweh whose words were placed in his mouth

[6] The *logos* of the Greeks drew its life from the idea of orderly gathering, and recognised speech as the critical arrangement of words: an understanding in which emphasis falls upon the content of speech rather than upon actual speaking. *Logos* continued its penetrating and explanatory function, denoting insights into the nature of the world and man's place here, and later rose to heights of metaphysical reality. But its chief task was to express the Greek supposition that within and through the world and all its components dwelt a norm assisting man to self-understanding in his cosmic environment. Knowledge of the norm included obedience and fulfilment. In face of his death Socrates says. "I am and always have been one of those natures that must be guided by reason, whatever the reason may be which upon reflection appears to me to be the best; and now that this fortune has come upon me, I cannot put away the reasons which I have before given: the principles which I have hitherto honoured and revered I still honour" (*Crito*, 46 b/c, trans. by Jowett).

The *logos* was definitive and obligatory for genuine human life. It became the fundamental fact of all life, the deepest, undiscoverable ground of the soul, enfolding within itself and indwelling all things. Broadly speaking we may say that by *logos* the Greeks emphasised the *articulate* element of *dabhar*, while its *energetic* principle moved Hebrew consciousness more profoundly. As viewpoints these have been said to be antithetical, but as emphases in man's awareness of the world they must surely constitute an instance of complementarity.

(Jer. 1:9), to engage in the creativity and destructiveness of the Lord. Prophetic utterances bore the hallmark of their origin, "Thus saith Yahweh"; and collections of oracles were introduced as "The word of the Lord" (cf. Hos., Zech., Mal.).

Thus the relationship of *nephesh to dabhar,* of the prophet to his word, is enveloped within a larger whole; and the word which rested upon the prophet's personal relation to Yahweh now becomes the word of Yahweh himself (cf. Isa. 2:1; Mic.; Zeph.), the extended personality of God. We may say that in the Hebrew awareness of the world, anyone who encounters the living Word, adopts it and allows himself to be "characterised" by it, becomes a different person.

This movement in which the mystery of being unfolds in Israel is not confined to the prophets but has its counterparts in the priestly and humanist traditions. Priests are mediators of the Law which, also, is a word:

> For out of Zion shall go forth the law, and the word of
> the Lord from Jerusalem.[7]

Torah, or teaching about God, inherits more than documentary status and is regarded as a power-nucleus with wider applicability in time and space than any one particlar prophetic utterance. The Ten Words of covenantal significance do not need to be retrieved from far-flung hiding places, for they also are in people's mouths and hearts to be fulfilled or to destroy their possessors with the bone-burning fever of their unspokenness. The interchangeability of *torah* with *dabhar* in the psalm (Ps. 119, *passim*) says that the dianoetic quality of the one mingles with the dynamic force of the other. Once creativity and the force of

[7] Isa. 2: 3 (RSV).

188

life reverberate in *torah* and *dabhar* alike, both participate in shaping and sustaining the world. By the word of Yahweh were the heavens made, the first-begotten *torah*, agent of the world's formation, lights up primeval darkness and spells out life everywhere.

The wisdom literature of the humanists in Israel was dominated by a godly fear so practical as to concern itself with men's skills and conduct of daily affairs. Such wisdom was highly prized, and some men ranked it as oldest of all and present at the world's formation. This feeling finds expression in the Book of Proverbs where wisdom, or *hochmah,* feminine and personal, speaks for herself:

Yahweh possessed me in the beginning of his way, before his works of old.
I was set up from everlasting, from the beginning, or ever the earth was.
When there were no depths I was brought forth; when there were no fountains abounding with water.
Before the mountains were settled, before the hills was I brought forth:
While as yet he had not made the earth, nor the fields, nor the highest part of the dust of the world.
When he prepared the heavens I was there: when he set a vault upon the face of the deep . . .
Then I was by him, as one brought up with him; and I was daily his delight, rejoicing always before him.[8]

Precise linguistic comparisons are not required to observe where these three tributaries—*dabhar, torah* and *hochmah* —rise or reach the sea. Their origins remain obscure, but their confluence is the river of life whose depth and nature is freshly apprehended in the personal Logos whom men subsequently identify with the historical Jesus.

[8] Prov. 8: 22–27, 30 (G. A. F. Knight's translation).

That which was from the beginning, which we have heard, which we have seen with our eyes, which we have looked upon, and our hands have handled, of the Word of life.[9]

The vital energy which imbued matter, the soul which spoke within and from the material world with human accents is now articulately "full of grace and truth." The sublimity and unconscious power of the world achieves emotional intensity, is "made flesh," and piercing man's inmost parts, penetrates the hitherto inaccessible depths of the material world to reveal within a habitable concavity of furnished awareness. The mercurial essence of matter under sensory observation, the illusory dimensions of its mysterious façade and its enigmatic features have been divined.

The Hebrews, it seems, were not enamoured of "world reason," nor did their messianic expectancy focus attention beyond the human, yet their sight, hearing and touch of Jesus pressed them to heap upon him qualities hitherto invested only in the Word of prophecy, of Law and Wisdom herself. Their earlier values are neither dismissed nor annulled but serve a personal category in which they are fulfilled. The new affirmation of the nature of the world is not an enlarged concept but a living person; and then not a traditionalist, but one in whom all received values are present in a new way to confirm the personal nature of things: who crowns with life the concept of the inwardness and the outwardness of matter. The heart of the energy which is the world and the content of all that had gone before now become tangibly and lovingly present. The vast multiplicity of things, hitherto dumb or relatively inarticulate, are now sensitively and intelligently articulated in him: he is the essence and hypostasis of their implicit potency,

[9] I John 1: 1, (AV).

190

the concretion of "matter" and "spirit." All things are summarised in him, for "what was made, was life in him." He is our new awareness of the nature of things, a new category for the appraisal of the world, the new key to the nature of man's home.

In modern writing Pierre Teilhard de Chardin's visionary apprehension of "Christ in matter" is perhaps the most powerful expression of the theme of this chapter. His autobiographical account, formally attributed to a soldier-friend long buried near Verdun, seeks to explain how "the manifold universe took on the likeness of Christ." Pondering the question which hides here, his eye was entranced by a picture of Christ which hung from the wall of a church he was visiting. The outlines of the figure began to melt into their background, without, however, losing their own definition. Surfaces changed to fields of force which radiated to infinity. "The whole universe vibrated" without destroying the individuality of any single thing, while nervous lines of light threaded paths through all substance. The luminous simplicity of Christ's eyes became infinitely complex upon closer study: reflecting fire, tenderness and passion, "manly majesty," "imperiously pure," a bottomless well of fascinating light, intense beyond comprehension. Then veiled with tears the vision faded to leave its precious residue of conviction which Teilhard has sought with diligence to confirm in all our minds:

I live at the heart of a single, unique Element, the Centre of the universe and present in each part of it: personal Love and cosmic Power.[10]

[10] *Hymn of the Universe* (New York: Harper & Row, 1965), p. 54.

11

The Essence of All Things

> So from the ground we felt that virtue branch
> Through all our veins till we were whole, our wrists
> As fresh and pure as water from a well,
> Our hands made new to handle holy things,
> The source of all our seeing rinsed and cleansed
> Till earth and light and water entering there
> Gave back to us the clear unfallen world.
>
> *Edwin Muir* [1]

> *For the created universe waits with eager expectation for God's sons to be revealed. It was made the victim of frustration, not by its own choice, but because of him who made it so; yet always there was hope, because the universe itself is to be freed from the shackles of mortality and enter upon the liberty and splendour of the children of God.*
>
> *St. Paul* [2]

A DECISIVE INFLUENCE upon the Hebrew sense of destiny was exerted by the view that soul and body are the inwardness and the outwardness of a man, and that each person extends beyond his physique to embrace his family and to penetrate his property. His well-being, or salvation, included the extensions of his personality, so that deliverance for the whole man meant deliverance from every kind of ill. His religion strongly affirmed this world, and was con-

[1] Openings lines of "The Transfiguration," *Collected Poems, 1921–1951* (New York: Grove, 1957, and London: Oxford University Press).

[2] Rom. 8: 19–20 (NEB).

ceived of practically as responsibility for communal existence here and now, without promise of a transcendental destiny for the "soul," compensated only by intermittent and faint expectation of bodily revivification.[3]

In joy of deliverance from slavery, and fear of the antagonisms of life, the Hebrews became engaged in a covenant with Yahweh. And if we say that the covenant involved the blessing of Yahweh and the obedience of Israel, his protection and his people's service, this contractual appearance must not obscure the permanent, personal relationship between them; they were bound together by "steadfast love." But once a community has entered upon a covenant promising conditional well-being, the impact of political and natural environment offers a tremendous challenge to its faith. In face of hunger, poverty, homelessness and humiliation, it would be possible for some men to abandon the practical aspects of their faith, and rather than see it founder in the midst of much adversity and failure, they would maintain it by transferring the fulfilment of its promised salvation to another world.

The Hebrews did not shrink the garment of salvation by immersing it in otherworldly reference and meaning; they allowed it to remain exposed to the turmoil of this world, and sought to envelop within it the whole of their natural environment. Thus they interpreted their destiny in the broad terms of a unity of personal life with that of their surroundings, and recognised a direct relationship between disasters which appeared from physical and political sources and the transgressions of personal existence. For

[3] Cf. R. Martin Archard, *From Death to Life* (Edinburgh: Oliver and Boyd, 1960), a study of the development of the doctrine of the Resurrection in the Old Testament.

example, the prophet Amos not only envisages the political downfall of the kingdom of Israel, but asks its inhabitants to interpret adverse physical phenomena such as drought and blight as auguries of an all-inclusive judgement upon their way of life (Amos 4:6–8). And although the relationship between man and the earth is expressed in terms of destruction rather than well-being, so that words of comfort contained in prophetic utterances are often regarded as suspect, the fact that judgement could involve nature along with man seems to imply a corresponding unity in well-being.

On this reading of events political nemesis overtook the Hebrews when they were swept eastwards on the receding tide of Babylonian invasion. The painfulness of exile was eventually gladdened by return to their homeland, but their foreign experiences have often been judged to have forced their abandonment of any concept of salvation which included natural environment in favour of apocalyptic hopes which left this world to its ruin. This view implies that the Hebrews reformulated the account of their destiny in other-worldly terms, and certainly within the tangled skein of apocalyptic literature strands of pessimism are abundantly visible.

Belief in a righteous God, fostered within prophetic tradition, helped to determine the concept of "the day of the Lord" as one of judgement upon mankind, while prophetic analysis of Jewish life led to the conclusion that "the day of the Lord" would be one of darkness rather than light. These sombre predictions, however, did not drain life of meaning, but tended rather to add dignity and seriousness to men's choices and behaviour.

Apocalyptic literature has this prophetic root, and its imported leitmotifs do not eradicate its Hebrew character. Resurrection life in a new heaven and a new earth is to be

194

lived *in the flesh;* the pessimism which conceives of this world as unfit for the realization of the Golden Age is accompanied by the neighbourly yet paradoxical optimism which anticipates its advent here:

And I will transform the earth and make it a blessing,
and cause Mine elect ones to dwell upon it: [4]

Apocalypticism has often been denied symbolic value by those who understood it to be historical prediction. Myths about the beginning of the world, however, have revealed more of their permanent value for being divested of their "literal truth," though myths concerning the end of the world have not shared equally in this edifying denouement; so despite the relatedness of beginning and end, the disclosure of the character of man's destiny has not been permitted to complement that of his origin. Seeking to penetrate the broken surfaces of things the apocalypticists declared the unity of cosmological with human events. Despairing of all finitude they continued to find hope in the wholeness of divine purposes, so that inability to affirm the eternity of the natural world of sensory experience did not mean that they abandoned it to destruction, but understood it rather to be included in the saving processes of their progenitorial covenant. This paradox of the negation and affirmation of the natural world is present also in the Gospels. C. H. Dodd drew attention to it in *The Parables of the Kingdom:*

We seem to be confronted with two diverse strains in the teaching of Jesus, one of which appears to contemplate the indefinite continuance of human life under historical conditions, while the other appears to suggest a speedy end to these conditions. A drastic criticism might eliminate the one strain or the other, but

[4] I Enoch 45: 5 (R. H. Charles's translation).

195

both are deeply embedded in the earliest form of tradition known to us. It would be better to admit that we do not possess the key to their reconciliation than to do such violence to our documents. It may be possible to find a place for both strains if we make full allowance for the symbolic character of the 'apocalyptic' sayings. The symbolic method is inherent in apocalyptic.[5]

Apocalyptic despair of this world does not, then, constitute an outright denial of the earlier inclusion of environment within the saving processes of the covenant, for it is overarched by hope of a *transformation* of the whole of creation.

This hope and despair are set out in peculiar imagery. The power of things to persist both structurally and vitally in time, over against chaos and disease, is attributed to spiritual beings: the creative forces to the good, and the destructive to the evil. Christianity has understood its founder to have mastered the powers of this demonic world, though the acknowledgement of his victory has sometimes been interpreted as a denial of the existence of its forces! So sweeping and proud a denial can hardly effect more than a formal separation of man from the mysterious inner depths of natural life. The phenomena explained by spiritual presences surrounding and invading man's life have not surely vanished from the earth, so that what was once attributed to the influences of personal or semipersonal beings is still experienced in the breakdown of individual integrity within the mass of men, or has come to be expressed in the idiom of the sciences: in the language of psychology and the biological disciplines, and in the theories of heredity and determinism. The myths of spiritual beings, of "the prince

[5] (New York: Scribners, 1936), pp. 104–5.

of this world" and his demon entourage, symbolise what is chaotic and discordant in the structure of existence: natural catastrophe, sickness and anxiety, enmity between human beings, distress in creation, the disparate phenomena of nature; in a word—things as they are compared with that world order of which men dream and which they believe to be their destiny.

The "clear unfallen world" of the beginning, the myth of paradise, bears this eschatological connotation. Man's condition is set within a framework of destiny. His actuality is a becoming. His *implicit* destiny in the myth of the fall, with its ramifications in the natural world, is spelled out in the myth of the restoration of paradise. This paradise-motif was not obliged to await an age in which apocalyptic literature became fashionable; expressing as it did an elemental human longing, prophets and psalmists also gave it forms appropriate to their literary genres. Isaiah, for example, pictures an idyllic reconciliation in which the enmity between animals of different species is superseded by peace, and the inadvertence of children among creatures normally dangerous brings no injurious effects. This peaceful order is attributed by the prophet to a world immersed in "the knowledge of the Lord" (Isa. 11:6–9; cf. chap. 35).

Ezekiel draws a similar picture but extends the hope of restoration from the world of animals into the kingdom of plants, and joins the fruitful earth with man's knowledge of the Lord as a deliverer from slavery and exploitation (Ezek. 34:25–30).

What these men contemplate does not vary in principle from the covenant at Sinai, but exceeds it cosmically in breadth of validity, so that Hosea, who also speaks about the congeniality of vegetable and animal life, grounds his

197

symbolism in a renewed covenant of *nature* with Yahweh (Hos. 2:18–23). No doubt, an impersonal view of the essence of matter, or of the nature of the world, renders preposterous Hosea's suggestion, but on that appraisal of the earth as personal in quality, which we have sought to make, his word enters the realm of rationality with wisdom and insight.

This prophetic symbolism, enfolding the earth with the destiny of man, was later focussed in the image of the Holy City, the New Jerusalem,[6] in which superfluousness of sun and moon as sources of light in face of the divine glory suggest the overcoming of the antithesis of the natural and the divine, while the multitudinous paean of celestial praise is shared both by "living creatures" and by "every created thing in heaven and on earth and under the earth and in the sea, all that is in them" (Rev. 5:13, NEB). And this ecumenical song bears symbolic testimony to the undiminished apocalyptic hope of nature's inclusion within the processes of salvation.

The writers of the synoptic Gospels implement this Hebrew heritage in testimony to Jesus. They breathe apocalyptic air. Sensing the mysterious conception of the new earth, seminally present in Jesus, they portray him as victor over the demonic powers of the world. Those powers, which had hitherto held all nature in thrall, now lie writhing and broken; the day of the ecumenical song has dawned; men stand upon its threshold. The cosmic significance of Jesus does not yet find conceptual form, but the worlds of nature and of the spirit are one kingdom only, of which he is master; and to those who wish to perpetuate the aberrant divorcement of the two spheres, Jesus is recorded as saying:

[6] Cf. A. D. Galloway, *The Cosmic Christ* (London: Nisbet, 1951), pp. 33–34.

'Is it easier to say to this paralyzed man, "Your sins are for-given", or to say, "Stand up, take your bed, and walk"? But to convince you that the Son of Man has the right on earth to for-give sins'—he turned to the paralyzed man—'I say to you, stand up, take your bed, and go home.' And he got up, took his stretcher at once, and went out in full view of them all (Mark 2:9–12, NEB).

So what the apocalypticists had symbolically portrayed the synoptic gospellers report as event and actuality within the dimensions of their personal experience. Renewal of the spirit and healing of the body are not unrelated movements; there is no wholeness for man without restoration for nature by virtue of their mutual enfoldment.

The directness of the Gospel reports and their compara-tive freedom from deduction hold memory's door ajar upon events, so that it is left to other New Testament writers to draw out their implications and to conceptualise the nature of the service Jesus performed.

St. Paul looks in this direction and descries the world with eyes of apocalyptic ambiguity; his despair of the here and now contends with his hope of its restoration. His synonymous use of the phrase "this world" with "this age" (e.g., I Cor. 3:18–19), and the powers or "princes" which were said to dominate it, link closely the created world with man's predicament in it, and emphasise a despair with which we then associate remarks which might describe re-treat from the world, retirement into himself, and rescue of a metaphysical sort while "this world" hastens to its end. But alongside this picture of disintegration St. Paul is aware of processes of upbuilding, and he sees a world—compris-ing nature and man—which is both theatre and object of salvation.

If we conceive of ourselves as existential unities and are

199

concerned with wholeness and deliverance from all that isolates and divides, then hope and faith must take account of our roots in nature and embrace the physical world. If we regard ourselves as essentially divisible, soul from body, then hope must fasten upon escape from flesh and the earth, and faith reach out towards wholeness of a metaphysical kind.

The spiritual aristocrats of St. Paul's day felt obliged to dissociate the evil of creation from the goodness of God. Matter they regarded as the principle of evil. And when it became impossible to reduce communication with the world to an ascetic minimum, they cultivated a peculiar indifference to phenomena which permitted them to treat the world as they liked. Their preference sometimes led them in unrestrained pursuit of natural impulse, but dissociation of the evil world from the good God was effected in their minds by the belief that there must be some effluence of deity. From its central fulness or totality of power, they said, deity germinates, and from the first generation a second evolves, and as the series increases the divine element in each generation grows successively weaker. Thus the world was ruled and created through a shadowy hierarchy of angelic mediators who, though graded and recognised by a cybernetic nomenclature, were often deceptive caricatures of the fulness they represented. But in the Gnostic mind they bound the finite with the Infinite, and by the same token held both apart.

The pressures of this spiritual ecology evoke from St. Paul a conceptualisation of the life and passion of Jesus whose historical achievements he sees as invested with cosmic significance. Compared with Gnostic anxiety to escape the contagion of evil by dominating matter and evading its toils, St. Paul sees Jesus, by character and action, embodying the essence of the universe: Jesus represents and epitomises, initiates and completes the nature of the world whose energies from man to the farthest star bend towards reconciliation. What had been veiled in abstraction is now unrestrictedly open to view, for the character of the universe is summed up "in Christ" through whom it has been created and moves upon its reconciliatory way (Col. 1:15–20).

The apostle's language naturally reflects the cosmology of his time, but his words of exaltation simultaneously reveal his understanding of the essence of the world. It is this: the abstract energies which enliven all things meet together and acquire personal features in Jesus. Everything is gathered up into him (Eph. 1:10). The forces of nature and history and the elements of what has since been designated as "the phenomenal-noumenal world" are concentrated in him, and shown to be personal. He is the source of universal life, its center of development, the mainspring of its motions and its principle of coherence. All the tones of the universe resonate within him. He is the beginning and goal of creation; everything emerges from him and converges upon him; he is its point of emanation and in him its harmonious climax is a *fait accompli*.

In this way the pessimism of apocalyptic expectation is held and contained within a more generous vision of cosmic reconciliation; [7] but simultaneously and unavoidably St.

[7] It is impossible to move from this visionary apprehension of the nature of things without observing a contemporary reflection of its glory in the intense and resplendent image of cosmic finality which appears in W. H. Auden's "Anthem for St. Matthew's Day":

"Praise ye the Lord,
Let the whole creation give out another sweetness,

201

Paul must express a doctrine of matter to the effect that "the world is charged with the grandeur of God"[8] which "flames out" in Jesus. In his description of the essence of things the Word is not mentioned, but the idea of the Logos clearly informs his thinking. With greater firmness, perhaps, the Fourth Gospel asserts that "through him all things came to be; no single thing was created without him. All that came to be was alive with his life" (John 1:3–4, NEB), but adds nothing to that which is already implicit in St. Paul's terminology. His Letter to the Romans introduces an unexpected element of destiny in which he sees the physical universe involved, and in correspondence with his faith and hope for mankind he declares that the natural order is also contained within man's wholeness, and will share "in the liberty and splendour of the children of God." In this astounding measure the language of faith dignifies the material world and binds it to man's future.

Yet biblical testimony to the essence of things is most succinctly expressed in that understanding of Jesus as divinity plunged into matter in order to redeem it. The doctrine of the Incarnation, primarily regarded as under-

---

Nicer in our nostrils, a novel fragrance
From cleansed occasions in accord together
As one feeling fabric, all flushed and intact
Phenomena and numbers announcing in one
Multitudinous oecumenical song
Their grand giveness of gratitude and joy,
Peaceable and plural, their positive truth
An authoritative This, an unthreatened Now
When in love and in laughter, each lives himself,
For united by His word cognition and power
System and order are a single glory
And the pattern is complex, their places safe."

[8] "God's Grandeur," quoted from *Gerard Manley Hopkins, A Selection of His Poems and Prose,* ed. W. H. Gardner (London: Penguin, 1953), p. 27.

girding man's "spiritual" existence, affirms both his roots in matter and the personal nature of the world. "Through your own incarnation, my God, all matter is henceforth incarnate." [9] As a consequence of this evaluation of Jesus, which moves into sharper focus with his own reference to a piece of bread as his body, the Christian Church has set at the heart of its worship small elements of matter which have never ceased to give offence.

In the mystery of the Holy Mass the religious emphasis undoubtedly falls upon concepts of offering and sacrifice. The presentation of bread and wine upon the altar is ultimately understood as the offering-up of Jesus Christ to God, and the involvement of the worshippers in this sacrifice. When, however, it is said that "Christ is present at the august sacrifice of the altar . . . above all under the eucharistic species" [10] and that the Eucharist "contains in a permanent manner the Author of grace Himself," [11] in whatever way this faith be celebrated liturgically, or conceived of philosophically by the Church, in ascribing to matter the reality of Christ it acquires a cosmic dimension and also reflects an authentic biblical understanding of the nature of the world. In spite of crude contrasts between soul and body, and false antitheses of spirit and matter as good and evil, in its doctrine of incarnation Christianity is able to speak of matter as holy, which the practise of the Roman communion affirms by means of transubstantiation.

[9] Pierre Teilhard de Chardin, *Hymn of the Universe* (New York: Harper & Row, 1965), p. 24.

[10] *On the Sacred Liturgy*, Encyclical Letter (*Mediator Dei*) of Pope Pius XII, 20th November, 1947 (New York: American Press, 1954), Section 20.

[11] *Ibid.*, Section 131.

203

The proverbial stagnation of oriental peoples was attributable in part of their understanding of the sacredness of nature. Its "desacralisation" among occidental men released forces of enquiry which have not ceased to drive us along unpredictable ways of scientific advancement, so that immense technological structures now rest upon a *secular* view of the world.[12] The world is now a field of human exploration and endeavour from which the gods have been sealed off. All the consequences of the secularising of nature have not yet reached fruition, but the judgement that matter may be utilised without consideration for the fate of mankind and the earth as a whole is seen to be fraught with extreme hazard. Nature had to be desacralised, or "disenchanted," in order to advance the humanisation of man and his physical environment, for the technical use of nature is also a revelation of its mystery. What is called "secular" cannot be a "godless" part of life, but rather the matter-of-factness of all things *alienated by man from its own virtue and bounty*. It is the potentially holy which awaits "the manifestation of the sons of God," and meanwhile suffers eclipse and frustration till man shall recognise its depth and wholeness.

[12] An intriguing exception to this thesis appears in Japan where a generation ago a technological civilisation had not divested itself entirely of animism. In 1935, under the auspices of the Tokyo Hat Dealers Association, Shinto ritualists read memorials to old hats, by which they were said to acquire a pathetic yet genuine dignity. A hat dealer who was questioned said, "If it were not for hats getting old and shabby and giving a chance for a next generation of new and fresh head-gear, we dealers would have poor business, so it is only right that we should show appreciation to the spirits of old hats. During their lifetime of service many hats have acquired personality, and all should be treated with due reverence." In the same year a meeting of gratitude to the telephone was held at the Tokyo Central Telephone Station, attended by officials and employees, when the hard-worked apparatus received the thanks of the assembled company. (Frederic de Garis, *Their Japan* (Yokohama: Yoshikawa, 1936), pp. 176 and 196.)

The biblical category of matter and man, described as the Word, or Logos, disregards the external world as an abstract entity, satisfactorily defined by science and philosophy, and bestows upon matter a personal meaning and destiny. It refuses to deal with the world as it reacts to cold scientific prodding and analytical investigation, but prods man himself, seeking to focus and deepen his human response to the whole of environment. The category of "the Word" is a momentary beam of light which searches man's inwardness; its "heart-rending" disclosures penetrate simultaneously the opaqueness of the world which it seeks to dissolve; it asks of objects their royal secret, and seeks to illumine their structures from within, and to show us "a new creation." It is also true that this category of "the Word" does not finally yield to rational analysis, but invades the realm of rationality by nourishing a logic of survival; for it does not wish the atom to catch fire or history to end in the triumph of reason and the agony of the species. It must be seen and must stand in its own light and may be judged by its ability or inability to augment life, to make for greatness, and to humanise the world.

Since the appearance of man upon earth there can have been no *absolute* nature, but only the world interspersed with men's artifices and in process of humanisation.[13] We are so interlocked with our physical environment that even our explanations of it are at the same time transformations of it. The entire assemblage of energies, creatures and things which make up our sensible surroundings constantly interacts with us and is never unambiguous of meaning. Simone Weil contrasts a mother sewing a layette for her

---

[13] The concept of "nature" is alien to the Old Testament in which it has no independent status, but rather an event-character, and lives, like man, not by a given structure but in covenant with Yahweh.

unborn child with a female convict in a prison workshop who is also sewing. The attention of both women is absorbed by similar technical problems while "a whole gulf of difference" lies within their occupational similarities.[14] Matter may weigh us down or uphold us, degrade or ennoble, threaten life or sustain it, become a source of weariness or exuberance; but its "nature" and effects will be determined by our relationship with it.

Through a personal universe one may have to tread with unaccustomed delicacy and humility, but it will not suffice for human beings to conform to nature or to regard it as unalterable by virtue of its sacredness. To overadapt oneself is to succumb to the limitations of things, while mere reaction to the provocation of environment by exploiting or subjecting it to a master-slave relationship is a dialectic of descent toward the subhuman. In a personal universe our affinity with things does not permit us to enjoy freedom without according it to matter. If material things cannot be liberated from man's parasitic interest and stupid infatuation, and from the frenzy of his accelerated productivity, he himself shall not taste freedom. *Extra* naturam *non salus est!* A personal universe demands that we treat the world in such a way that our thinking about it and our handling of it release within us the power of becoming human, and elevate the status of things themselves through the treatment they receive.

Those questions posit a false antithesis, therefore, which ask whether the biblical restoration of all things is to be regarded as "subjective" or "objective"; whether rehabilitation will be accounted for by our changed perceptions and attitudes of mind, or accomplished irrespective of men. Our

[14] *The Need for Roots* (London: Routledge & Kegan Paul, 1952), p. 91.

relation to the natural world is not of a purely external character. It is a dialectic of exchange and *ascension,* enunciated with great clarity within the framework of biblical thought. The proclamation that "the Word became flesh," of which the eucharistic symbols are crowning instances and paradigms, affirms this ascensional force of the world in which matter is charged with the dimensions of Christ and shares in the power which reconciles all things.

The bright strand of cosmic redemption drawn through biblical literature not only indicates an affinity and destiny common to man and things, but also attributes to matter as to man a function within the salvation-structures it describes. It shows nature participating with man in the processes which make for wholeness, reflecting the value of his life, and sharing in the power which augments it.

12

Dust and Immortality

Immortal life is life full of content. But already this life has its content, value and aim in itself. Every moment of life is fulfilled being and of infinite significance; . . . Each moment is a draught which drains the cup of infinity.

Ludwig Feuerbach [1]

Man is mortal. That may be; but let us perish resisting, and if the void await us, do not let us so act as to deserve it.

E. P. de Sénancour [2]

> *My heart is by dejection, clay,*
> *And by selfe-murder, red.*
> *From this red earth, O Father, purge away*
> *All vicious tinctures, that new fashioned*
> *I may rise up from death, before I'm dead.*
>
> *John Donne* [3]

THE COMMON DESTINY of man and the world, and belief that their essence is "of the Word," press upon Christian teachings which lie beyond the scope of this enquiry. Yet

---

[1] *Sämmtliche Werke*, I (2nd ed.; Stuttgart: Frommann Verlag, 1960), pp. 88–89: ". . . *unsterbliches Leben ist inhaltsvolles Leben. Aber schon dieses Leben hat seinen Inhalt, seinen Werth, seinen Zweck in sich selbst. Jeder Augenblick des Lebens ist erfülltes Sein, von unendlicher Bedeutung: . . . jeder Augenblick ist ein Trunk, der bis auf den Grund den Kelch der Unendlichkeit ausleert.*"

[2] *Obermann, Lettre* xc (Paris: Bibliothèque-Charpentier, 1901), p. 412: "*L'homme est périssable. Il se peut; mais périssons en résistant, et, si le néant, nous est reservé, ne faisons pas que ce soit une justice.*"

[3] "The Litanie, I: The Father," *The Complete Poetry and Selected Prose of John Donne* (New York: Random House, 1941), p. 248.

the apocalyptic optimism of the Bible with its climax in the New Testament, asks importunately for some response to questions about man's future and the content of the category of "the personal."

What is man's future in the light of his relationship with matter? How shall his common destiny with the material world be spelled out? Does the picture of cosmic redemption suggest unambiguously that matter and men are destined for life beyond each man's decease in time? If, on the one hand, man's destiny is shared with his physical environment and, on the other hand, linked with categories reflecting "another" world, may these natural and transnatural destinies be viewed in other than mutually contradictory light? According to the New Testament, to be saved is the same thing as to have eternal life; in which respect does the word "eternal" distinguish the life it qualifies from life measurable in years, terminating in death? Can we valuably affirm that "the other world" is our own world seen in a particular light? In reply to Stavrogin's question, "You've begun to believe in a future eternal life?" can we frankly join with Kirillov and reply, "No, not in a future eternal life, but in eternal life here"? [4]

On the basis of our understanding of the common essence of man and things may the substance of those Christian doctrines which speak about "another" world be contained within this world? May those events which lie along a supposed line of chronological time be translated into energies which fill to overflowing the private time-space of our inwardness? May we so assimilate belief in an "after-

---

[4] Fyodor Dostoevsky, *The Possessed* trans. by Constance Garnett (New York: The Modern Library, Random House, 1963), p. 239.

life" that the support it gives us does not take a form of encouragement springing from the hope of "unending" life, but rises from an enlarged and intensified awareness of that "eternal now" which is the life we know?

In response to the challenge presented by the common destiny of man and things, shall we courageously replace belief in an endless future with belief in eternity? Shall we accept the fact that we are creatures originating in a ground that is eternal in quality, and are destined to return to it? And that in the interval between our appearance and disappearance eternal life is the goal? In what way is the conduct of life related to its goal? To these questions the remainder of this chapter is directed.

Palestinian Judaism offers no evidence of belief in a state of salvation to be experienced in a transcendent realm beyond time and space. The apocalyptist in the Book of Revelation envisages a recreated universe in which the barriers keeping heaven and earth apart are broken open, and heaven *descends* to assist at the blessedness of earth. It is also worthy of note that the concept of immortality barely infiltrates the Bible, and then only with diffidence and uncertainty.

Every doctrine of immortality, it is said, implies a tragic preoccupation with death, and this nervous form of "ultimate concern" may well be a part of the ground from which the doctrine derives nourishment. When, instead of closing the door upon this life, death opens it upon another, the creative tensions within our persons are reduced, and our sense of being at home in the world is undermined. By the same token also it is feasible that privation of the hope of immortality increases man's availability and concentrates his presence here. Indeed, Albert Camus insisted that mortality in a meaningless world infinitely increased the value of life, and that to remove the finality of death was to deprive life of its gravity. He called Pindar to his aid, who said,

> O my soul, do not aspire to immortal life,
> but exhaust the limits of the possible.[5]

Kierkegaard was similarly minded when he described immortality as judgement rather than the continuation of life after death.[6] Speculations about immortality demand proof. Understood as a task, the essential challenge of immortality is not whether men survive death, but what they do in respect of the personality they hope may survive.

This Kierkegaardian note echoes in the work of P. T. Forsyth, who colourfully reproaches those who have turned the doctrine "from an imperative task to a leisurely theme." It troubled him that a vocation had become an enigma, that a matter of conscience and duty had suffered such change as to be a thing of poetry and speculation, and that the hope of immortality had been turned into a search for occult assurance. He insisted that life was not a stream which we had reason to think continued flowing after its disappearance round a certain bend, nor that it was an inevitable movement towards the future. "Do not waste time asking if there is a coming eternity; ask, what must I do to give effect to my present eternity; ask, how shall I be loyal to the eternal responsibility in me and on me?" [7]

[5] *The Olympian and Pythian Odes*, ed. C. A. M. Fennel (Cambridge: Cambridge University Press, 1879), p. 163. *Pythian* III, lines 61–62:

μή, θίλα ψυχα, βίον ἀθάνατον
σπεῦδε, τὰν δ'ἔμπρακτον ἄντλει μαχανάν.

[6] *Christian Discourses* (New York: Oxford University Press, 1961), p. 212.

[7] *This Life and the Next* (London: Independent Press, 1946), chap. entitled "Immortality and Present Judgement," pp. 44–47.

With respect to the literature of the New Testament it is noticeable that the ambiguities of "body and soul," "flesh and spirit," particularly as they occur in discussions about life after death, have confused understanding of the mention of immortality made there. The appearances of "body and soul" are not basically equivalent to the Greek σῶμα and ψῡχή, but reflect the Hebrew *nephesh,* which epitomises the total man and does not sharply differentiate between life and death. "Body and soul," therefore, despite their appearance, represent far less concern with what happens after death than they might convey to those for whom ψῡχή is detachable from σῶμα.

It is inexact to suppose that St. Paul uses the terms "flesh and spirit" synonymously with "body and soul." His words for flesh and spirit are σάρξ and πνεῦμα, and do not indicate the body-soul dualism of the Greeks. They represent respectively the powers of sin and charity: the "fleshly" man is in process of disintegration; the "spiritual" man grows in the wisdom and stature of love.

No doctrine may be rightly assessed without reference to those who accept it; its content will reflect those nuances of sentiment which strongly characterise the culture within which it is held. The reading of immortality into the New Testament has been encouraged and confirmed by that false individualism which mistakes the distinctions between men for separateness, and loosens the bonds which hold mankind together. An "atomic" individualism allowed men to substitute for the cosmic character of redemption a private eschatology in which the restoration of all things atrophied to concern for one's own survival; and instead of participating in a transfigured world of men and things, the resurrection of Christ was made to function as an assurance that the

212

"faithful soul" would be introduced through death to enduring life and celestial splendour.

As a display of wealth in poverty's face accentuates human distress, so in an age when the world has been "loosened from its sun" and now strays through "infinite nothingness" the security of an overelaborate creed spreads despair. Have we not suffered the nausea induced by theological opulence which ineffectively hid a want of character? When the question is seriously asked whether nihilism is not a heritage of the Christian understanding of God's transcendence, it is perhaps time to suggest that a theology which reflects courage in face of life's hazards and uncertainties, though less grandiloquent, may evince more power to sustain men than that which announces its hold upon another world. For too long now the myths of the Christian religion have been divorced from nature and tempered by history to a degree which endangers their life and ours! Where they have been accepted as literally historical they have been lifted from the depths of life to float upon its surface as targets for scientific and philosophical marksmen. But this exposure, together with the appeal of Marx's dialectical and creative materialism, the fruitful but alarming relationship of man with his physical environment, and the exploration of human personality in depth, have stimulated in biblical theology a power of growth and the claim to some living space in the midst of dubious or scornful neighbours.

An appropriate justification of this view may be seen in the briefest survey of the concept of the Kingdom of God and the movement of meaning which has taken place within it during this century.

Although it became clear that the term "Kingdom of God" referred to sovereignty rather than territory, and that the happiness of men was involved in the rule of God, the question of the nature and presence of this Kingdom in time and space, or beyond them, provoked the most varied speculation. Albert Schweitzer believed the life and teaching of Jesus to be dominated entirely by the eschatological expectation of a Kingdom which lay wholly, though immediately, in the future. But this view of an essentially supernatural Kingdom was unable to maintain itself in face of indications given by Jesus that the Kingdom was in some sense a reality in the present. Liberal theologians, whose unreserved love and admiration for Jesus stopped short of worship, believed the Kingdom to be an ideal for remodelling society through the media of social reform and political action informed by Jesus' ethical teaching. But then the apocalyptic language of Jesus, spoken in an atmosphere charged with similar hope, made it too difficult to believe that this linguistic medium, in those circumstances, would have conveyed a nonapocalyptic message of social evolution; and temptations to deny the validity or to transform the content of apocalypticism in his message were mainly withstood.

Thus the "Kingdom of God" was widely acknowledged to be an apocalyptic concept, but into it a question of time was introduced. C. H. Dodd maintained that the most characteristic Gospel pronouncements on the subject declared unequivocally that the eschatological Kingdom was a present fact, that the future had powerfully broken in upon mankind in the ministry of Jesus, and that the eschaton was *realised;* any implied future coming of the Kingdom of God did not refer to this world but to an ultimate fulfilment of the Kingdom in a transcendent order beyond time and space. However, this transcendent element ran counter not only to the expectation of Jesus of a future state of affairs characterised, for example, by a reversal of the present order, but also to the clearly stated apocalyptic hope of a transformed earth as the final scene of the eschatological drama. So, from the records alone, it seemed impossible that the question of the Kingdom of God as present or future could be resolved.

The apparent contradiction between presentness and futurity was gathered together by J. Jeremias in the phrase, "eschatology in process of realisation" (*sich realisierende Eschatologie*), and the emphasis of the discussion moved away from the apocalyptic, supernatural character of the Kingdom to consider in what respects it might now be present or future or both!

The suggested resolution of the antithesis in a "timeless kingdom" was not generally upheld, and the tension between present and future was described in terms such as a present reality working towards a future consummation, or a present fulfilment bearing within it the certainty of future promise. Oscar Cullmann used his now famous metaphor of the Second World War and likened the relationship between present and future to that which existed between D-day and VE-day. In the present a long-promised eschatological salvation is known at a personal level within and through the ministry of Jesus; in the future this salvation will reach its cosmic fulfilment through an act of God described in imagery such as that which clothed the Parousia.

Here the discussion was valuably assisted by the consideration that the moral teaching of Jesus was an integral part of his understanding of the Kingdom, that it was not immediately directed towards the world at large, but pointed to

215

the eschatological community whose obedience was a manifestation of the presence of the Kingdom. Yves Congar pictured this situation in a way reminiscent of Cullmann. He saw the Church as "the maquis of the world": under distressing conditions, *already acknowledging the reign of the liberator,* and awaiting the fulfilment of its struggle for freedom in a landing "from outside." Thus the ethics of the Kingdom were seen to be interwoven with the eschaton.

This dialectical engagement of present with future in the Kingdom of God was sharply interrupted by Rudolf Bultmann, who took the witness of Jesus to mean that the Kingdom was dawning but *not yet present,* and that it was apocalyptic rather than something which developed and grew. Disdaining nationalistic types of expectation Jesus aligned himself with apocalyptic antecedents, but modified them by challenging his contemporaries to substitute for their distant hope of supernatural events and a transhistorical life, the recognition of his own person and ministry, not as messianic, but as signs of the "end" and of the imminence of the Kingdom.

Such imminence, according to Bultmann, is not temporal but existential: the Kingdom does not come in the mere course of time but, as retroactive power from the immediate future, creates in men a crisis of decision for or against the total phenomenon of Jesus. Reading twentieth-century philosophical terms into first-century thought forms, Bultmann explains that inasmuch as decision is of the essence of being human, a positive choice in the crisis created by the activity of God turns imaginary or potential into real existence. He therefore envisages Jesus translating apocalyptic hope of the imminent end of history into a challenge to accept him and his ministry as expressions of God's last word before the "end," and in this way welding dynamically into unity the proclamation of the Kingdom and its ethical demands. Bultmann's disciples modified his emphasis upon a wholly future Kingdom breaking in upon men in the ministry of Jesus by showing that Jesus not only called for decisions about the future but also announced the present as a time of salvation. There is an essential difference between a present which leads to a future and a present which bears already the marks of the future: in the second instance the future is *within* the present, and is in some sense "fulfilled." Inasmuch as there is a reciprocal relation between the content of time and the experience of duration, so that καιρός cannot be severed from χρόνος, Jesus anticipated a consummation in the future of what had happened in his ministry; but those aspects of his message which look beyond crises of decision to the actual rejoicing of men within the grace of God indicate that he was concerned less with "times and seasons" than with people themselves who provide the content of history. He was not attempting to discuss the "consummation" of world history, but to grapple with the "end" of history for every man, with each person's life or death. Thus present and future constitute an *existential* dialectic; entry into the Kingdom of God becomes the pivotal point of each man's destiny; and beyond that point of entry the future is present in each man's obedience, demanded and given, within the freedom which love creates.

This existential result has drawn attention to concepts of time and the nature of the "end." In contrast with our linear view of time, which moves towards a climax, the Hebrews thought of time as a series or rhythm of *moments filled with events*. Agricultural festivals were connected with saving events and become "history." God's saving ac-

217

tions were henceforth "remembered," though historical memory was not concerned with stretches of time as such, but with making present those time-events in which men believed that God had acted to spare them. Old Testament prophets witnessed to the faith that contemporary events were likewise endowed with saving quality, and dared to proclaim a future, climactic event in which God would save his people. Prophetic eschatology, however, treats not of the end of time or history, but of a future act of salvation which will be more decisive than those recollected from the past; indeed, one which will be final.

The concept of the Kingdom of God represents this further and final saving event which breaks into the world and men's experience. Apocalypticists subsequently attached to these prophetic simplicities an elaborate and bewildering superstructure of hope and expectation, but their mystifying achievement still rests upon belief in a divine intervention in history and the salvation it will bring.

One of the many apocalyptic motifs was a royal display of warlike power by God on behalf of his people, and in the synoptic Gospels this holy war is wrested from the future to become a decisive encounter with Satan, whose kingdom is regularly "plundered" in the release of victims of demon-possession. The battlefield assumes dimensions of personal inwardness, and the arena of eschatological conflict becomes a theatre of operations "within" and "among" contemporary men and women whose lives are challenged by Jesus and by his disciples.

In the awareness of the prophets God's presence in all events was supremely important, and they measured history by this norm. In apocalypticism time ran its predetermined course according to a divine plan; events were not significant in themselves, but only in relation to an envisaged climax; seers could therefore portray history with mythological imagery and search for signs of the end in order to calculate its proximity. Jesus rejected apocalyptic calculations of history in favour of a prophetic awareness of all times in which God manifests himself unexpectedly to men and calls for their response to his presence; he concentrates upon men's personal existence as the medium of God's appearing and declines the sphere of external events. To be sure, the in-breaking of the Kingdom of God is not without "signs": there is Jesus himself with his works of forgiveness and healing. But these phenomena offer no proof: Jesus is unrecognisable except to faith, while miracles and pronouncements are not necessarily attributable to God's kingly activity. As the Kingdom of God breaks into history and human experience, it is present only to those who interpret events in a particular way and commit themselves in trust to the authoritative personal power revealed there.

Of the Kingdom of God as future Jesus offered no description except to say that it contained judgement and hope, and would vindicate the values he had set upon life. Beyond this he counselled watchfulness and maintained the tension between present and future in personal existence. His warnings of the Kingdom's sudden and "unobservable" appearance in their midst helped men to ride the temptation to loosen the tautness between the times with external expectations of cosmic catastrophe, a heavenly realm and life after death, and to withstand the inclination to destroy the mystery of its presence with the descent of a heavenly being. Tension is a man's native element, and to do justly by

219

the teaching of Jesus he must hold fast to the conviction that the Kingdom of God *comes and is to come* within history and individual human experience.[8]

This shift of emphasis within the concept of the Kingdom of God from otherworldliness to the tensions within the personal life of man is not an isolated phenomenon, and may be seen as a movement concurrent with that of an increase in zeal for existentialism.

Kierkegaard affirms that the sole reality known with certainty by any man is his own existing self; and the knowledge of the world which forms part of his total experience is really interpretation. Man's existence, he says, bears an odd sense of responsibility, for while no man brings himself into the world he is nevertheless responsible for the shape of his existence here: he is free to frustrate or implement the forms his life may take in its growth and vigour. This freedom is each man's responsibility; it is not a concept but an existential datum. Answerableness is woven into the fabric of being human, and it is exercised in the continuous moment we call "now," which gives significance to past and future. It is impossible to freeze this "fragment of eternity" into immobility, for freedom and responsibility place upon us the burden of choosing, and each choice issues in a new self that did not previously exist. Thus the characteristic dimensions of the self are freedom and responsibility, time, choice and becoming. Subsequent existentialist thinking accentuated the view that the force of gravity in personal life pulls towards the future; that human beings are an anticipation of their own possibilities, and exist in advance

[8] For the greater part of this survey I am indebted to the work of Norman Perrin, *The Kingdom of God in the Teaching of Jesus* (Philadelphia: Westminster, 1963).

of themselves by grasping situations as a challenge, not to be what they must be, but to become what they may become. Human being consists in aiming at what it is not yet, and in reaching out beyond itself; and in this sense of going beyond what is immediately given, men are said to transcend themselves. Thrust irreversibly into the world, they find that their understanding is vitally connected with the *things they understand.* Within the necessities of this given world they discover a freedom in which they may strive to actualise their own possibilities. But however much they project themselves into the future and seek to make it real in the present, their self-projection never outruns the boundaries of this world. Men are inseparable from the world, and their understanding of it reflects an apprehension of themselves.

Much of the movement of meaning in the concept of the Kingdom of God may be attributed to the pressure of this kind of thinking on the part of the existentialists, and we must ask whether or not the interpretation it has produced is justifiable. The most recent reading of the Gospels cannot be final, and it cannot express exactly what the biblical writers sought to define and interpret in their accounts and testimony, yet an existentialist content to Scripture may be justified in view of the following consideration.

Our own intellectual tools may never release from the literary forms of ancient times the precise meanings which once inhabited them, while faith itself cannot be distilled from even the nicest accuracy of detail. Men's religious awareness, which included an awareness of the world, was different from our own, so that our categories of interpretation may never restore its actual temperature and quality to us. But we stand in the same stream of events and may become contemporary with the past; indeed we may change its value for ourselves. But unless we assume that the ancients stood in a closer relation to truth to which we must revert, our lives can hardly depend upon the "correct" interpretation of a now partly hidden religious awareness of life. Having overcome a literary "fundamentalism" we dare not succumb to a fundamentalism of interpretation. As life impinges upon us and the nature of our need becomes articulate, we may read the documents of our religion and examine the strata of interpretation which constitute our tradition, and permit ourselves to be addressed by the persons and situations of the past as they *now* confront us within the patterns of our thinking and self-awareness. And at this point of impact or meeting we may accept as revelatory, and therefore as authoritative for us, that which now confirms and increases our humanity: but the personal power from which we may draw enthusiasm and the courage to be, will be conceived of in terms that do not trespass spatially beyond the boundary upon which, eventually, men return to dust.

Is there an awareness of death within which we grasp that it both is natural to man and ministers to the wholeness of his life? Can we apprehend that life is not simply "rounded off" by this mysterious horizon, but that death operates as a retroactive and formative power throughout our days and, far from devaluing life, is one of our precious possessions?

We understand its biological necessity: that individuals disappear for the benefit of the species, and species vanish in favour of the ever changing forms of life. But is death more, in human experience, than the stark biological fact which limits individual becoming?

It is perhaps important to notice the significant difference

222

between the fact of death and the process of dying. My dying is internal to myself, so that in order to die to myself I must somehow continue to live. My death as an accomplished fact is external and public. I do not consciously participate in it. In the lives of my acquaintances it may be a private event, but it is one of which I am oblivious!

Death itself is an undiscovered country, but the process of dying is not unfamiliar to us. Our experience of the deaths of others brings death home as part of our own immanent future; and because it is not necessarily linked with old age, it is near to us during our lives. Understood in a general way the subject may well be one of interest and curiosity:

> Death is something that we fear
> But it titillates the ear.[9]

But the deaths of people more closely related to us by love or work speak of matters beyond the strictly biological, for we participate in the experience of their dying with a poignancy which the thought of our own demise does not contain.

We participate in a friend's last hours. When his life has ebbed and calm arrives, and the living person is no longer there, our compassion is relieved, for unlike the act of dying, death itself is not accessible to us. Living people are never quite beyond the range of sympathy; the dead are. The sudden absence of the person we may interpret by the measure of our susceptibilities, but never as annihilation. Death as an absolute end is an empty concept, which we do not experience. D. H. Lawrence, a confidant of that death "which lies between the old self and the new" attempts a

[9] Louis MacNeice, "Bar-room Matins" (written in July 1940). *Collected Poems, 1925-48* (New York: Oxford University Press, 1963) p. 200-1.

statement of nonbeing which necessarily reflects no light at all:

> And everything is gone, the body is gone
> completely under, gone, entirely gone.
> . . . .
> It is the end, it is oblivion.[10]

Biologically every organism pursues its life, exhausting its energies. When vital processes in man reach their end the "self" disappears, yet the body remains for a time, allowing imagination to fill up the vacuum of nonbeing. But the spiritual person has vanished, the broken communion within which we were contained threatens our own existence, for each man's death is unique and universal. His death "diminishes" us. Through his absence we experience the qualitative nature of separation; and a new dimension of life is opened within. But the pulse of this awareness, sensitive to the richness of the person by whose death impoverishment has come, is stimulated only by love and attachment. The personal significance of his death is then built into our life and has a character-forming effect upon us. Once we accept the diminution of our existence and its impoverishment by the death of another, his significance comes home, fructifies and enriches us by its conditioned immortality there.

To participate in the entire human condition we must permit ourselves to be exposed to dying. Either we appropriate death or we never live to the full. Praying for its maturation within us, Rilke asks that it shall not hang "sourly and greenly" upon the tree of our life, like fruit unwilling to ripen, but enlarge us with the meaning, love and need it bears:

[10] "The Ship of Death," *Selected Poems* (London: Penguin, 1950), pp. 128 ff.

For we are but the leaf and the skin.
The great death which each one has within
is the fruit around which all revolves.[11]

The task of appropriating another's death, of dying with him, is that of transforming what is the enemy of "endless" existence into nourishment for being human. Death provides both biological framework and spiritual definition to life; it gives form to life, illumines its awareness and sharpens its pleasure, so that our personal destiny is to translate its fatality, by absorption, into greater humanity and freedom.

Martin Heidegger has described human being in its entirely as "being-to-death" (*Sein zum Tode*), and it is true that our life faces death. But can it therefore simply be affirmed that human being is an existence towards death? Is it not rather an existence towards self-realisation in which death may become a ministering power? Death in its biological inevitability, absorbed by love, is the necessary food of a mature personal existence. It is this faith which turns death into a threshold of resurrection and bears us over into an enhanced kind of life.

Man is not being-to-death, but being-through-death. He is called neither to despair nor to behold death's mystery and squander its energies in mere curiosity and impossible objective affirmations. He fulfils himself by the acceptance of his own death; and by living in its light, he may live beyond it. In the growing structures of existence man's awareness of himself as person has heightened the poignancy of death, yet its anguish cannot now at long last become

[11] "Das Stunden-Buch: Das Buch von der Armut und vom Tode," Rainer Maria Rilke, *Sämtliche Werke* (Insel Verlag):

> *"Denn wir sind nur die Schale und das Blatt.*
> *Der grosse Tod, den jeder in sich hat,*
> *das ist die Frucht, um die sich alles dreht."*

incomprehensible as though death were without honour, gravity or creative power. In self-affirmation we desire to press beyond the limits of time, and so we do, but not into endlessness. We may surpass time's boundary in a qualitative existence which the New Testament calls "eternal life." Faith in personal survival is the shape man frequently gives to this ontological imperative, yet he has often spent its virtue upon an unknown country. Given the hospitality of love, death's creative energy begets full-grown men; it is its finality which may make us whole. Therefore:

> No waiting for, no gaze at things celestial,
> just longing to give even Death his due,
> and humbly train ourselves on the terrestrial
> so that his hands shan't find us wholly new.[12]

At the heart of sacramental existence within Christianity lies the acceptance of death, reversing the dictum of Jesus who called his death a baptism, by proclaiming baptism a death, and the communion of bread and wine a voluntary and joyful repetition of the acceptance of its judgement and grace. Its invitation to discipleship bears the same connotation: the challenge daily to carry the cross is a call to embrace the sentence, brought home by the death of Jesus, as a beginning of eternal life. Thus death is the supreme festival on the road to freedom; the transcendent is not infinitely remote but immediately at hand; life's beginning and end are not simply its extremes, but lie at its heart and centre. And in this way it appears that man's destiny is wedded to the world of things.

[12] *Ibid.*, p. 255:

> "*Kein Jenseitswarten und kein Schaun nach drüben,*
> *nur Sehnsucht, auch den Tod nicht zu entweihn*
> *und dienend sich am Irdischen zu üben,*
> *um seinen Händen nicht mehr neu zu sein.*"

Epilogue: Vision and Glory

Thinking is learning all over again to see, to be attentive, to focus consciousness; it is turning every idea and every image into a privileged moment.

Albert Camus [1]

It is certain that the divinest consolation is contained in humanity itself . . . but our eyes should be a shade more perceptive, our ears be more receptive, the taste of a fruit should be absorbed more completely, we should be capable of enduring more intense smells, and be more alert and less forgetful when we touch and are touched—so that in our most immediate experiences we might find consolations which are more convincing, stronger and more valid than the most overwhelming sorrow.

Rainer Maria Rilke [2]

HUMAN BEINGS are engaged in two adventures: one descends into the depths of time and another explores the breadth of space. The first is concerned with the discovery of inwardness; the second is an engagement with the external world; and danger attends each adventure if it be undertaken to the exclusion of the other. If exploration in breadth suffocate his concern with depth, man's spirit be-

[1] *The Myth of Sisyphus* (New York: Random House, 1959), p. 20.

[2] *The Letters of Rainer Maria Rilke and Princess Marie von Thurn und Taxis-Hohenlohe,* trans. Nora Wydenbruck (London: Hogarth, 1958), pp. 144–45.

comes shallow and his person dispersed in matter. If his pursuit of breadth be neglected for engagement with the depths, his self is dispersed in dreams; for man is called upon to be related to time and space, to "possess" both the world and himself.

In the chapter entitled "The Essence of All Things," this dual relationship was represented in the perspective of a reconciled cosmos, but such pictures tend to acquire an "objective" reality which they do not actually possess. When we speak of the future in this external fashion it appears to assume characteristics of inevitability which, in fact, are not automatically assured, but may be thwarted by chance and prejudiced by human dereliction. By the law of increasing entropy man's ultimate future is considered to be one of annihilation, while the sting of this death is thought by some to have been removed by Teilhard de Chardin's observation that the increasing complexity of matter has been accompanied by an increase in its conscious elements and in the levels of consciousness attained.[3] But none can predict how the internal propensity of matter to unite and to increase in complexity and consciousness may manifest itself in circumstances not yet given. This uncertain condition of man which cautions us not to solidify our concepts of the future will discourage some, but incite others to "realise" their eschatologies here and now, particularly when they recognise that by these "objectifying" methods religious thinking has often embezzled for "the Beyond" forces which would augment man's life in the present.

[3] *The Phenomenon of Man* (London: Collins, 1959), p. 287, where Teilhard describes this observation as "the law of complexity and consciousness."

This theological transformation of spiritual energies into future states is a source of impoverishment and constitutes a devaluation of life. Among the variety of reasons which may account for it we have questioned beliefs which assume that soul is detachable from body, and that behind this visible world there hides "another" world different from this.

By these dualistic tokens matter itself has been granted less than its due, and this underestimation of its nature is our misfortune. Beneath the apparent inertia and passivity of matter lies an aggressiveness which insists upon compensation for our disregard of its vital character. Thus the material world has beclouded the transparency of our over-spiritualized love; it has permitted God to become an object of religious invocation, and a Being, now banished to remoteness, in whom the world is believed to exist.

In a formally religious way, then, people came to live in the antechamber of God's *name* abstracted from his reality, whence they called upon and sought to possess him. But his silences when so addressed have now evoked a new discretion. A namelessness is growing up between men and God. Just as the atom, once supposedly apprehensible as an object, has now been transformed into a world in miniature which we may no longer possess, and to which we may simply be related, so a namelessness of God has sprung into being. Because his name was abstracted from reality, the experience of the sensibility of his presence is being eclipsed by a new awareness of everything *sensible*. God has become ineffable; and in this unspeakableness his attributes are accorded to creation, to love and to death.

Our twofold adventure—into the external world of space and the inner infinity of time—obliges us to say that each sphere has its duty to the other, and that things silently impose their trust upon men. Physical environment is to be *absorbed* into ourselves and given an invisible life, for only as things external participate in man's inner experience may they achieve their proper status. Jean-Paul Sartre reminds us of the ambivalence of the alimentary metaphors—absorb, digest, assimilate—which relate to knowing, and adopts the alarming viewpoint that destruction itself is a form of appropriation.

The flames which burn the farm which I myself have set on fire, gradually effect the fusion of the farm with *myself*. In annihilating it I am changing it into myself. Destruction realizes appropriation perhaps more keenly than creation does, for the object destroyed is no longer there to show itself impenetrable.[4]

But the possibility of this consuming vision does not obliterate the reality of a *creative attention*. In a direction opposite from that of absorption and possession there flows a stream upon which our inwardness is borne towards the world. It is no longer jealously guarded against invasion, but projected into the open, out of its distinctiveness and false individuality into the whole. Endowing the outer world with inner fervour and granting inwardness to matter is to impose a new shape upon the world, to bestow upon environment its anticipated dimension: that is to say, by the degree of our own disentanglement, to communicate to things their awaited freedom.

Detached observation fails to reach out to things for their own sake; Sartre's spectator devours with his eyes; the *emotional* observer, *moving out* of himself, realises the qualities of things themselves. His granting of inwardness to things is

[4] *Being and Nothingness,* trans. by Hazel E. Barnes (New York: Philosophical Library, 1956), p. 593.

a penetration of matter by means of attention which engenders life.

An object lies inert and nameless by the wayside. Passing travellers scarcely notice it, and this fleeting perception rapidly fades from their minds. But one man focusses his attention upon it, and his looking is an act of self-forgetful concentration upon that which meets his gaze. He does not consider whether his immediate experience is painful or pleasant, objectively real or hallucinatory, expected or unexpected, like or unlike that which has confronted others. He does not ask himself whether this is the beginning of an act of love on his part towards a neighbour, or an occasion for doing good; for all these considerations would disrupt his attention and divert his thinking away from the object and towards himself. To imagine himself loving something for the sake of God, or reflecting that what he was about to do pleased God, would kill the creativity of the moment: even these reflections would deprive the object of inwardness, and would have the effect of abandoning it in the scale of being at the level of a useful or promising piece of matter. Such is the moment's sensitivity that, under the impact of a single thought of God, it would be destroyed!

Inasmuch as things are observed creatively in an act of self-renunciation, one man readily exposes himself and sees with a sacrificial eye. The moment of creative attention commands him completely: he has all he can do to concentrate upon the wayside object, to be diminished by the expenditure of energy such looking requires, and to be so far removed from himself as to become unaware of his own existence.

This moment of renunciation is equally one of engagement: he allows himself to be penetrated by the object; he

231

bestows upon it an inwardness which lifts it up and grants it a share in his life. And the actions which follow reveal the creativity of his attentive glance, for the inert, anonymous object is lifted into freedom and a life of its own; indeed, under the eye of rescuing love the object acquires personal characteristics. In a Gospel account the object became a man!

In a moment of compassionate attention things acquire a quality of existence which they did not previously possess. Being loved for their own sakes they inherit a share of man's freedom. A plot of earth may not develop human characteristics or be endowed with human feelings, though it may cease merely to be "real estate." It is granted a value in itself; its existence is promoted; and in the same movement the humanity of its promoter is enhanced.

This vision and sympathy eventually qualify the biblical phrase, "dominion over things." Biblical dominion breathes humility; its authority is filled with service; it does not masquerade in the vesture of servility in order to exert a false power over things. Its renunciation bestows a virtue that humanises the world, and its authority resides in a manifestation of the most sombre though sovereign glory, piercing the depths of existence, whence it raises to dignity and wholeness the entire world of man and things.

Index

Alexander, S., 103
Ambrose, 75–76n
, Amos, 194
Animals, 55, 57f
Animism, 204
Anselm, 69, 76
Apocalypticism, 194–95, 218f
Appleton, Sir Edward, 23
Aquinas, St. Thomas, 37, 46, 76, 81–82, 132
  and the natural world, 81–82
Archard, R. M., 193
Archimedes, 67
Aristotle, 41, 74
Armstrong, D. M., 60
Arnobius, 75n
Atoms, 65–66
Auden, W. H., 201–2
Augustine, 75n, 76

Bacon, Francis, 77, 100–101, 142
Baillie, John, 13n
Battelle-American Assembly, 48
Baudelaire, Charles, 23
Bergson, Henri, 69, 90, 103n
Berkeley, Bishop, 89
Bible
  / portrayal of nature, 180–81
  themes, 178f
Biran, Maine de, 60
Blake, William, 14, 174
Body and soul, 40f, 53, 212, 229
Boehme, J., 100–101
Bombard, Dr. Alain, 29

Bonnot de Condillac, E., 52, 57n
Bosanquet, Bernard, 37
Boulanger, J. B., 182
Brain, Sir W. R., 36
Brainwashing, 27, 30
Braque, Georges, 15
Brecht, B., 146, 150
British Association, 50
Brock, Edwin, 54
Bronowski, J., 14
Browning, Robert, 39, 111
Buber, Martin, 54–55, 64, 72–73, 80, 112–13, 144, 175
Bultmann, R., 216–17
Burney, Christopher, 31
Byrd, Admiral R. E., 28–29

Campbell, Roy, 11
Camus, A., 90, 120n, 151f, 210, 227
Cancer, 50
Capelle, W., 41
Carlyle, Thomas, 14
Cassirer, E., 116n
Cézanne, Paul, 15
Charles, R. H., 195
Church fathers and the natural world, 75–76
Cleghorn, S., 182
Condillac (see Bonnot)
Congar, Y., 216
Consciousness, 35, 88, 103, 124–25, 183
Cooley, C. H., 170n

233

236

237